Rodeo Champions

Don Gay on Red One, NFR 1976. *Photo by Dave Allen*

Rodeo Champions

Eight Memorable Moments of Riding, Wrestling, and Roping

Larry Pointer

University of New Mexico Press
Albuquerque

Design by Milenda Nan Ok Lee

Library of Congress Cataloging in Publication Data

Pointer, Larry, 1940–
   Rodeo champions.

   Bibliography: p.
   Includes index.
   1. Cowboys—United States—Biography. 2. Rodeos—
United States—History. I. Title.
GV1833.5.P64   1985   791'.8 [B]   84-20826
ISBN 0-8263-0787-6
ISBN 0-8263-0798-1 (pbk.)

To
Pat

Contents

Illustrations

Preface

What is rodeo? Rodeo is sport, chills and spills and thrills of derring-do. Rodeo is pageantry, a "chunk of Americana," a Wild West show. Rodeo is big business.

Rodeo is all this. And much more simply, less. Caught on the edge of rodeo's fleeting images is a rare glimpse of the whole of Aristotle's *Poetics*; of a unity of space, time, and action: mortal man and primordial beast united in the dust to form ancestral sacrament to eternal spirit.

The Professional Rodeo Cowboys Association (PRCA) and the Women's Professional Rodeo Association (WPRA) sanction eight contest events. This book describes memorable moments drawn from each of the eight events. *Rodeo Champions* is the testament of the rodeo heros, man, woman, and animal, who lived Aristotle's *Poetics* on the edge of space, time, and action. It is their revelation of the whole, seen clear in the mirrors of memoir and action; indelible impressions of intense action, detailed to distill the immortal moment of the contest.

If in the action you are stirred, if you glimpse the immortal edge of here and evermore, and if you catch the rush of the ecstasy and the agony, the book will have succeeded.

Acknowledgments

To the champions of the respective rodeo events, Joe Alexander, Roy Cooper, Tom Ferguson, Mel Hyland, Olin Young, Jim Rodriguez, Jr., and Ken Juman, Jimmie Gibbs Munroe, and to John Quintana, Don Gay, and Denny Flynn, a very humble thank you for your patience and persistence in getting the story right. And to the equally important supporting cast, the people of rodeo whose shared recollections have contributed details of those times now turned to memory, a special thanks for setting the record straight. Their muster roll is long; many are referenced at the end of the book.

Gratitude is expressed to Bryan Lonski and his staff at *World of Rodeo*, and to Larry Jordan and the National High School Rodeo Association's *Rodeo Times*, for permitting me to offer portions of *Rodeo Champions* for the enjoyment,⁵ and constructive criticism, of their knowledgeable rodeo readers.

To Dr. Kristine Fredriksson of the PRCA Prorodeo Hall of Champions; to Chan Bergen and *Western Horseman*; to Bryan Lonski and Bill and Jo Smith of *World of Rodeo*, for ferreting out representative photographs; and to each of the photographers whose works illustrate text action, Dave Allen, Al Long, James

Acknowledgments

Fain, Jerry Gustafson, Bern Gregory, and Bruce McShan, the author is especially indebted.

To Luther Wilson and the editorial staff of the University of New Mexico Press, for writing guidance and editing of the final manuscript, deep appreciation is expressed.

To my wife Pat, and to so many others, thank you for the encouragement.

Rodeo Reflections

If I were to have chosen my rodeo beginnings, I don't suppose I could have made a better pick. In 1945, wide-eyed at five at the Bots Sots Stampede in Sheridan, Wyoming, the "World's Largest Working Cowboys Rodeo"—there, from the top of the grandstand, I could see forever. From the Big Horn Mountains to the horizon stretched a canvas of foothills and valleys, buttes, coulees, and cool grass prairie. On this canvas, history had painted a mural of Indians, mountain men, and cavalry men; ranchmen, horsemen, and remittance men; good men and bad men; Wild Westers and rodeoers.

Here once roamed the buffalo; the Crow, Sioux, Cheyenne, and Arapaho. Here ran the Bozeman Trail with its frontier forts. Here lay the remains of yellow-haired General Custer and his Seventh Cavalry. Here, the end of the Texas Trail; the range of the OW, PK, Padlock, the Antler and the Spear. Here, Eatons', where Teddy Roosevelt was treated to the bully working guest ranch, visited, by the blue bloods of Britain.

Here, on the lawn of the Sheridan Inn, Buffalo Bill held tryouts for his Wild West Show and Congress of Rough Riders. Here, before the turn of the Cheyenne Frontier Days, Shorty

1

Jennings staged early-day contests of range steer roping and bronc busting. And here, by Coffeen's Grove on the banks of Little Goose, in 1909 was born the Bots Sots Stampede, the Sheridan Wyo Rodeo.

Here was what rodeo was all about, to a tow-headed boy at the top of the grandstand. Those bleachers were built the year Wyoming adopted its famous bucking horse emblem, after the World War I symbol that Sheridan cowboy George Ostrom designed for his fighting unit, the 148th Artillery.

The place was right and so was the time, a time when patriotic pride ran high in Americans. World War II was over; our boys were home and we were celebrating, in the best Western way we knew how.

Rodeo will always mean this to me: a parade of cowboys and Indians, a drum and bugle corps, our soldiers come marching home. And at the county fairgrounds, at one o'clock sharp, bombs bursting, the flag floating in air. A cowboy band decked out in red shirts, white chaps, and white hats. A midget playing the piccolo. America.

And out front the twin ellipses, racetrack and rodeo grounds. A grand entry, a queen contest, and an afternoon program filled with riding, roping, bulldogging, ice-cold pop, and a wild horse race around the ellipse. The rodeo ellipse—and two poles, unseen, yet constant. Two invisible poles shaping the rodeo universe and the horse track beyond. An ellipse within an ellipse.

Looking back, now, at the age of forty-five, I wonder: has it always been there, this ellipse held in tension by its unseen poles? Did it find its form in man's time? Musing, I trace its succession back from rodeo arena to horse track, to Roman Coliseum and the bullring of Spain, back to the Olympic field of ancient Greece. What opposing forces created its magnetic field? East and West, man and Man, triumph and tragedy, life and death?

A flag is raised. A stopwatch is cradled in the timer's hand, thumb poised. Tension mounts, crackling in the air. All eyes are hypnotized in anticipation. A head nods.

Lightning flashes across the magnetic field.

The answer somehow must be found in that spark, glimpsed then gone in dim remembrance. If only it could be brought back, held still. Then, just maybe then, it could be seen clear and as a whole.

From the day I looked ahead at five to today, looking back from forty-five, what has passed between these unseen poles? Perhaps in the changes can be found clues to the mysteries of life in the rodeo ellipse.

When Sheridan's Ralph Buell broke into the big time of professional rodeo to claim the title of World Champion Bareback Rider in 1962, local interest in rodeo also reached out. At Cheyenne, at the State Fair in Douglas, or at the Midland Empire Fair at Billings, audiences could see a full slate of such world-class competitors as Jack Buschbom, Jim Shoulders, Harry Tompkins, John Hawkins, Casey Tibbs, and Eddy Akridge.

But even as these masters danced with balance and control, a revolution was forming in the ranks beneath them. It was because of, rather than in spite of, their exemplary styles that a new breed of performer sought new ways to beat them at the rodeo game.

In the postwar era of bareback riders you could tell a man's home range by the rig that he rode. The men of the midwestern plains rode a Charlie Beals rigging of the traditional style, patterned in the late 1930s when bareback riding went respectable as a rodeo event. These short-bodied surcingles with squared cinch irons and leather layered handholds were direct descendants of the first "bull rigs" fashioned for exhibitions in traveling Wild West shows.

The West Coast riders chose a Pete Dixon rig, deep-bodied

3

and stiff, with rounded D-rings and a hard handle laminated from rawhide. Using these rigs, the California boys began to experiment with ways to get by a bronc too tough to out-stout. Adhesive tape, first used in the 1940s, was almost universally in use by the 1950s. An added feature was Andy Miliate's piano-wire "rip cord," with its wooden handle, put into use in the late 1950s. When a ride was finished, either up-side or down, the taped-in rider just jerked on the rip cord to cut through the tape and set himself free.

The Rodeo Cowboys Association (RCA) had banned tape and rip cords by Ralph Buell's title year, but the bareback inventors had perfected an even better trap, the "pipe". Also the handi-work of Miliate, and of fellow Californian Tom Downey, the pipe was based on a Pete Dixon rig. The handhold was constructed of a metal core, to which rawhide was laminated. An application of fiber glass finished the pipe handle, Once hand-formed to a custom-tailored fit, the "pipe" held a hand like a vise.

In looking back down my thoughts, I can see that it was the times, the Buddy Holly, Elvis Presley, Jerry Lee Lewis times, that caused the genesis of the pipe. The pipe did not cause the revolution in bareback riding styles. The pipe was a tool, a new tool for a new breed of rodeo cowboy.

Even as the fairgrounds exhibit halls ceased to reverberate to the sounds of Bob Wills western swing and began to jump with the rock and roll beat, the old-time working cowboy on a rodeo lark found himself surrounded by a new generation of contes-tants. Many had never worked on a ranch.

Rock and roll found its rodeo parallel in "flop and pop," a wild, rear-over-backward-heel-in-the-air explosion of abstract bareback expression. Leaders of this new breed were Buddy Peak, the Mayo brothers of Grinnell, Iowa, and a lanky kid from downtown Omaha, John Houston. The wildest of the wild ones

4

was small Bob Mayo; Houston had the most lasting impact on the event.

With his Championship Rodeo Equipment enterprise out of Burkburnett, Texas, Jim Houston capitalized on a Dixon-Downey-Miliate rigging he had inherited from Dewey Dunaway, one of the early Bots Sots working cowboys turned pro. Houston rode his pipe to a brace of world titles. When the pipe was outlawed with the 1970 season, Jim Houston, now RCA bareback director, was ready with an opportune line of rigs with deep bodies, sloping D-rigs, and a rock-hard rawhide laminate handhold that wedged a rider's hand as tightly as had its fiber-glass-and-metal forerunner.

With his hand locked in, the bareback rider of the 1960s and 1970s could throw all caution to the winds. "Exposing yourself to the ground," they called it. "Out of control," the old breed would retort in denunciation. In response to changing styles, and a new generation of spectators who cheered the riders on, a new method of scoring necessarily evolved among the contestant judges. As "wild" became the dominant factor in a rider's score, balance and timing became passé. The flop-and-pop rider had to be out of time with the step and drive of his mount to be "in."

Two poles in the rodeo ellipse, the old breed and the new. Yet between these poles from time to time an exceptional ride will spark the gap. Old and new unite in allowing that when it happens, all the colors of the rodeo spectrum merge in an image so intense, its impression is seared forever in your mind. Such a ride was that of Joe Alexander and Marlboro, relived in this book.

Leaving behind for the moment the chute world of man versus horse, and wandering into the rope-box world of man and horse partnerships, another opposition becomes apparent in the rodeo arena. As a boy I only vaguely sensed it, in the differences observed: a fifteen-dollar bareback rig, chaps, and a pair of spurs in the war bag behind the chutes; an investment running upwards of fifteen hundred postwar dollars in rope horse, horse trailer, and the shiny V-8 vehicle standing in the infield sun behind the rope box. Devil-may-care grins of rough stock riders gave way to stern, worried visages of heavy responsibility in the roping world.

And between the two an uneasiness, more sensed than seen. A hard edge in the banter between the men at opposite ends of the rodeo ellipse; the rarity of those all-around men like Gene Rambo and Phil Lyne who contested at both ends. An aloofness was signaled in contrasts: the rakish hat and colorful shirt of the bronc rider; the roper's conservative dress and the ranchmen's crease in his Stetson. They were different, riders and ropers. I little knew why. But I often wondered.

Now, looking back forty years, I can see that there was a social distinction from one end of the arena to the other, a distinction between the haves and the have-nots. There was a caste system in early-day rodeo, even as there had been on the stockman's range. The hired hands of the range-cow outfit more often than not provided rodeo with its nomadic bronc-riding will-o'-the-wisps; foremen, ranchmen, and ranchmen's sons were the men who owned the horses, the trailers, and the shiny V-8's.

I've often puzzled over those differences, present still in a sport nearly a century old in the American West. Working cowboys were a world apart from the ranchmen in whose employ they rode. Theirs was a feudal culture, echoing the ante bellum South of plantation gentry and brush-popping Crackers; the landed colonials and their indentured servants; the land-grand hidalgo horsemen and natives on foot in New Spain. It was a social distinction steeped in the chivalry of Europe, between landed cavaliers and the peasant classes.

The distinction was blurred to me as a boy at the World's Largest Working Cowboys Rodeo. There, I was as apt to see a hired man on a borrowed horse as a ranchman's son mounted on an animal bearing the family heraldry on his hip. Hero of the local folk was Jess Thomas, foreman of the OW ranch, who bought his first brand-new car with his checks from the Bots Sots Stampede.

That time was money in the clocked events came as an early realization to Sheridan rodeo goers. At the first rodeo held at the fairgrounds, in 1931, the Bots Sots purse attracted the best of the early-day world-class ropers, men who first made their living by contesting their skills with the catch rope and pigging string. The calf-roping champion was Jake McClure of Lovington, New Mexico. His times, 17 seconds flat on the first run and 19.6 on the second, awed the 6,000 locals gathered for the show and placed him ahead of Bob Crosby, the "King of the Cowboys" featured in *Life* magazine. In third place was yet another champion of that golden era for rodeo, Richard Merchant.

The speed of the men was second only to the phenomenal getaway demonstrated by the rope horses. To the northern hands, who rode the wide circle at roundup time on long-legged, deep-winded thoroughbreds that traced their heritage to the cavalry remounts of the Indian wars, the squat, muscled, "bulldog" quarter horse of the rodeo arena, bred for early speed, was something else altogether.

In the postwar rodeos at Sheridan, calf ropers still followed the ways pioneered by Jake McClure and those first ropers. Either with a wide northern loop or with McClure's narrow rodeo circle, a calf was caught, the slack was pitched, and the animal was thrown by the mount's sliding stop. The horseman dismounted to his left, the natural side. He ran down the line to the calf, grabbed a foreleg, and tipped it over onto its back. Three legs were tied with the pigging string in three wraps and a half-hitch "hooey." By the 1950s, however, ropers were learning to duck under the rope to flank the calf down in the manner of Toots Mansfield, the champion roper from Bandera, Texas.

7

Then by the 1960s, ropers were beating the competition by a righthand dismount, pioneered by Oklahoman Shoat Webster back in the early 1940s. This last was a controversial move for the roping fraternity, and it caused nearly as much controversy as had the pipe in the bareback event. But time was money.

Undisputed champion calf roper by this time was Dean Oliver. Seven times between 1958 and 1969 he was the RCA World Champion. In three other seasons he placed second to only one other calf roper in the world. And he did it the natural way, from the left. It was a record to shoot at, for sure.

As with the bareback riding event, the pride of style in roping created a polarity of rodeo generations. And as Joe Alexander had done in his event, one man ignited the field between with a consistency that transcended controversy. That man was Roy Cooper.

Cruelty to animals became the issue to polarize the single steer-roping event in rodeo, the only other roping contest on the 1931 Sheridan Stampede program. It was townsmen against ranchmen, as humane societies caused state after state to outlaw the tripping of steers.

Steer busting, or fairgrounding, as it came to be called because of its association with early Independence Day celebrations, is one rodeo event that grows directly from life on the range. This true artifact is also unique to the culture of the American cowboy. As Scots-Irish and Anglo frontiersmen moved from the piedmont and pine barrens onto the plains of Texas, they came into contact with the longhorn, the mustang, the Mexican vaquero, and an open-range cattle culture totally alien to anything they had ever known in the cow pens of the Carolinas and Georgia. The Vaqueros roped their cattle with reatas of plaited rawhide. *Dar la vuelta*, to take a turn, was what they called the way they snubbed the line with a wrap around the saddle horn. Most often they roped in tandem, one at the horns, another on the heels.

In a hurry by nature, the Scot discarded the Spanish reata for sisal and manila "whale lines" and tied the free end hard and fast to the horn. Borrowing from the vaquero trick of *coleando*, somersaulting an animal by a hold on its tail, the Texas cowboys learned to trip steers with their ropes in the same fashion. Saddles were beefed up to take the strain, and the sturdier quarter horse came to replace the small Spanish mustang of the frontier in the cowboy contest.

Humane groups protested the event as barbarian, citing injuries to both cattle and horses. The ranchmen countered, demonstrating that if everything is carried out properly, no injuries need result. Even in Wyoming and the other states where the event remained legal, its popularity ebbed and flowed with the times. Only at Cheyenne did it maintain its standing, and even there it was abandoned from the last day of the 1909 contest until 1913 when the controversy had subsided. Team tying replaced steer busting during that period.

In 1931 at Sheridan the steer-roping event attracted many of the Cheyenne champions. Dick Truitt took the event with an average of 25.2 seconds on two steers. Behind him were Lloyd Saunders, Herb Meyers, and John Bowman, top flight Oklahoma ropers.

After the war, the Bots Sots Stampede dropped the event in favor of team tying, a range adaptation of the single-steer-roping contest. The team-tying variation that was popular among the working cowboy contestants at Sheridan involved a header and a heeler, both carrying ropes tied hard and fast. Once the header caught cattle and reined away, the heeler traditionally would approach from the right with a side-arm slap shot under the steer to snare a hind leg or two. The heeler then would turn his mount away from the action and the steer would be stretched out between the two mounts, each facing away from the steer. The header then would dismount and tie the downed animal.

The vaquero's "dally" style of team roping was not seen as a rodeo contest event on the northern plains until the late 1960s, when the Bots Sots Stampede finally went professional under sanction of the RCA. The Spanish custom was not readily accepted on the Great Plains, north or south. In Arizona and Nevada it began to be accepted by the 1920s, but it was largely a West Coast phenomenon that did not spread until organized rodeo experienced its growth explosion in the post-war years. When eighteen-year-old Jim Rodriguez, Jr., teamed up with the great all-around champion Gene Rambo win in his first world championship in 1959, steers were roped by alternate dally and team-tying tactics. Not until 1968 were all ten head at the National Finals roped under the dally contest rules, and that was an experiment in deference to the large contingent of California dally ropers. It was really not until 1973 that team tying finally was dropped as an NFR contest event. The polarity between Anglo and Latin runs deep in Western culture, and rodeo mirrored the split. Thanks to such men as Jim Rodriguez, Jr., racial and cultural differences slowly but certainly have been overcome.

From the roping boxes back to the bucking chutes, the Bots Sots Stampede program again drew attention to the pageant of man's victory over beast. Saddle bronc riding has been called the classic event of rodeo, as American as jazz in its point-counterpoint play of action, pure in its poetic motion. As Wyoming's license-plate silhouette shows the world, the state is expressly proud of its broncs and bronc riders. Area cowboys like Paddy Ryan, Bob Askin, Howard Tegland, Turk Greenough, and Doff Aber were househould words in Bots Sots Country. The animals, too, were known by heart, from the first nationally famous bucking horse, Steamboat, to Tipperary, Midnight, Five Minutes to Midnight, Hell's Angel, and the awesome big broncs of Leo Cremer's string, bred from fiery throughbred and huge draft-animal stock.

Rules and gear were standardized by the 1920s when the freak "bear-trap" saddles with outlandish front swells were outlawed in favor of the Committee rig of uniform dimensions. Then appreciation of the fineness and fine nuances of the event became akin to the appreciation of fine art. I would sit and listen in total rapture to the tales that were told of broncs and bronc riders, but the best that I ever did see was at Cheyenne in 1967 when Mel Hyland rode Reckless Red.

Cow cutting brought diversity to the rodeo program of the 1940s. Here was the only event open to women in the postWar years. At Sheridan, Alida Sage of the Triangle T often as not took home some of the prize money with her Texas-bred and educated cutting quarter horses.

Before the war there had been contest events for women in bronc riding, steer riding, and relay horse races. The ladies' bronc-riding event had been a popular contest at Cheyenne from 1906 until it was eliminated following the 1927 contest. At Pendleton as well as back east in the Boston Garden and Madison Square Garden World Series Rodeo, lady bronc riders either contested or rode in exhibition. In Bots Sots Country, the names of Fanny Sperry Steele, Prairie Rose, Ma Gibson, Bertha Blancett, Mildred Douglas, Brida Gafford, Bobby Brooks and Alice and Margie Greenough were almost as well known as were their male counterparts.

In 1936, with the birth of the rodeo contestant's union, the Cowboys Turtle Association (forerunner to the RCA), one of the negotiated items given up by the cowboys at the bargaining table was the sanction of women's contest events. In their place at New York, the rodeo producer substituted Texas society horsewomen performing equestrian displays, including a reining pattern that would grow after the war into the cloverleaf barrel race. From this event grew the Girls Rodeo Association.

The only cowgirl mentioned at the 1931 Sheridan contest was Tad Lucas of Fort Worth, Texas, the all time great trick and fancy rider, fancy roper, and pony express rider. When the barrel race appeared on the RCA program in the late 1960s, Albin Dygert challenged all contestants to a stopwatch showdown with his motorcycle. He lost. Chauvinism and chivalry are two invisible poles that have stood in the cowgirls' rodeo ellipse.

For entertainment appeal to spectators of all ages and nations, the rodeo business has contrived to offer exhibitions of skill and derring-do limited only by the imagination of their prolific creators. There have been, to name a few, chuck wagon races, relay races, wild horse races, chariot races; horses jumping automobiles, hurdles, and flaming barriers; wild cow milking; cowboys singing; goat ropings; trick roping; trick riding; steer undecorating and bulldogging.

The last of these, bulldogging—or steer wrestling as it is now known—possibly predates all of the rodeo contest events. Its roots run to the very dawn of civilization two millennia ago. The bull dancers of Minoan Crete performed a kind of bulldogging, steer wrestling was on the program of the ancient Greek Olympics. It is one of the forerunners of the bullfights of Rome and Spain. The steer-wrestling feats of the Greeks were not revived until the 1880s, when the black cowboy Bill Pickett began performing bulldogging exhibitions for public entertainment in Texas. In his performances for the Miller Brothers 101 Ranch Wild West Show, Pickett would dismount from the left, land on the head of a longhorn steer, sink his teeth into the soft lip of the animal, much as trained bulldogs had done in the English countryside, and throw his weight backward to pull the pain-crazed animal onto its side.

As the feat came to be contested in major rodeos, biting was outlawed in favor of overpowering the longhorn steers by physical might. A variety of wrestling holds evolved, culminating in the standard practices of today, as men became more proficient and *corriente* steers shrank in size from their massive longhorn progenitors.

Bulldogging was an all-time favorite event at the Bots Sots Stampede, from the very beginning when Jack Kerscher of Miles City tipped over two big, slab-sided longhorns in 8 and 11.6 seconds, respectively, to best the all-around champion, Dick Truitt. Truitt himself was also famous for his buffalo wrestling exhibitions, as was a modern-day Sheridan steer wrestler, Fred Larsen, who performed the feat for the movie *Buffalo Bill and the Indians* in the 1970s.

To me as a young boy, a smooth bulldogging run was awesome. Here was Hopalong Cassidy, professional wrestling, Superman stopping a freight train, and a magic show with a physics lesson in the power of the fulcrum and the lever, all rolled up in one. To blink was to miss the event, it happened so quickly. And I saw enough misses, hoolihans, and Bots Sots grunting and groaning contests to appreciate the lightning fully when it struck.

At the professional shows in the area I learned to appreciate the cowboys' own reverential inflections when they mentioned names like Homer Pettigrew, the McCrorey brothers, and later, John W. Jones. As I worked with college hands and the smaller steers of modern rodeo, I was able to appreciate, too, the rapid rise in the professional standings of such collegiate cowboys as Frank Shepperson of Casper College, Tom Ferguson of Cal Poly, and my own Fred Larsen. I also gained an abiding respect for the wonders of video slow-motion replays. Blinking *was* missing it all; seeing was an education in appreciation.

It was Fred Larsen who introduced me to the finer points in the manly art of bull riding. Since that fateful May day, bull riding's unseen poles in the rodeo ellipse, the haunting and the haunted, have made their presence felt. I bucked off the sorriest of the sorry. I enrolled in Jerome Robinson's bull-riding school. I bucked off some more. Then, between the launching and the landing, for eight brief seconds I glimpsed immortality. I'll never be the same again.

But in distinguishing form from shadow in the whirling vortex of bull-riding action, I learned most from seeing: my own Britt Givens capturing the Northern Rodeo Association all-around or taking the All Indian title; watching PRCA-found friends riding to glory at the NFR. From it all I could piece together just what it takes for a man and a bull to combine honest try into stellar performance.

Bulls, I have come to learn, possess two measures of excellence: power and speed. Men must muster in action-reaction kind. And that is the why of the Tale of Two Toros in this book. The power of V61, the fluid grace of John Quintana; the gyrating speed of Oscar, the catlike reflexes of Don Gay.

In the spark is struck the whole. This is the truth of rodeo.

Alexander the Great

Wind-driven showers spattered the men in yellow slickers and crumpled straw hats as they sorted the bucking horses for the final day of the 1974 Cheyenne Frontier Days. Each year since 1911 it had rained on this rodeo known as the "Daddy of "Em All." Bolts rattled in latches, dry hinges moaned, and plank gates clattered as the broncs jostled against the fence and balked in a well-rehearsed pantomime of fear. At the staccato of whistles and hoarse shouts the horses were peeled from the bunch one by one.

Dodging past the arm-flopping stock tenders, the paint horse Marlboro crowded into line in the alley to the chutes, his hooves flicking mud into the air. Down the line, slide gates popped open and shut. Eight horses filled eight mire-speckled chutes for the first even on the program, the final go-round of the bareback bronc riding. Scenting the electrifying air of excitement, the chestnut paint pawed the ground and kicked at the chute, sending tremors through the ancient structure. He had been here before.

Marlboro was a bareback bronc, a professional athlete in the purest sense. Driven in from the shortgrass range of eastern

Colorado in 1955 and sold to the Beutler Brothers' rodeo-pro-ducing combine, the paint gelding was a bucking horse to be reckoned with. Every year he had been to the Daddy Of 'Em All; eight times the cowboys had nominated him to the National Finals. Marlboro loved his work: he bucked, with enthusiasm and no little cunning. He was twenty-three, at the pinnacle of his prowess, and today he was on an emotional high. The cool, moist breeze was intoxicating; the grain in his sleek belly was an elixir to his blood.

Chute boss Buster Ivory draped a sheepskin-padded flank strap over Marlboro's hips. The bronc humped his back and kicked at the strap tickling his sensitive flanks. Using a piece of wire bent into a claw, Buster drew the flank strap under the gelding's belly and secured the ring in a quick-release latch, then moved down the line to the next bronc.

Behind the chutes the bareback riders were in various stages of preparation. Rosin chunks were crushed and rubbed onto rig-ging handles with gloved fingers until friction heat created a tacky union. Latigo straps were liberally lubricated with baby powder. Yards of adhesive tape were looped from forearm to upper arm, securing elbows in figure-eight wraps. Cowboys loosened up with exercises, stretching taut limbs, backs, and groin tendons. Other riders stalked back and forth in a trance, stopping periodically to flex neck muscles or to lash out a boot, toe turned out at a right angle, in a spurring lick at an imagi-nary bronc.

Of the Cheyenne finalists, reigning World Champion Joe Alex-ander had drawn the Marlboro horse. Alexander was far in the lead, headed for his fourth crown (and there would be more). Here, however, on this last overcast afternoon of the Frontier Days, Joe was behind in total points and up against the stiffest of competition. As he eyed the paint in the chute between him and the battleground of the arena beyond, Joe didn't relish the impending eight-second war. Four times the quiet cowboy from Cora, Wyoming, had squared off with the heavily muscled bronc. Marlboro had rued the day in their first set-to, at the National Finals. It had been a bitter lesson, and Alexander knew his score this day would have to be dragged out of the wily Marlboro.

Joe crouched beside his canvas war bag and emptied its contents. Spurs bound together by their straps; thin-soled walking boots, the cowhide scuffed to suede; horsehair riding pad; goatskin glove; bareback rigging; lightweight fringed chaps; and an old woolen sock stuffed with chunks of amber rosin—these were the tools of the bareback trade.

Joe's rigging was shaped to conform to a horse's withers. A Jim Houston pattern handcrafted by Raymond Hulin, the body had neolyte and rawhide sandwiched between thick leather. Reinforcing strips of rawhide were riveted around the body ends where sloping metal D-rings were sewn in for the cinch. The design allowed the rigging to rotate on the D-rings like a rocking chair, lifting the body front with each snatching jerk from the bucking horse.

The stiff handhold—built up with laminated rawhide strips—was shaped to fit Joe's left hand, with the handle twisted to the right. The left front bar was riveted to the top of the rigging body, the right bar attached under the body. The handle sloped to the rear where the base was bolted through the rigging. Here, Joe had added a thin leather strip to the body, tailored as a wedge for his palm and little finger. The handhold base was set to the right of the centerline, allowing Joe to tuck his riding arm close to his body with his wrist straight, in line with the tremendous forces exerted by a stout bronc like Marlboro.

Joe unwrapped his rosined goatskin glove from the handhold and passed the rigging to his traveling partner, saddle bronc titlist Bill Smith of Cody, Wyoming. With the quiet deliberate motions of a man familiar with handling livestock, "Cody Bill" eased onto the platform on the backside of Marlboro's chute and lowered the pad and rigging to the horse's back, behind the prominent withers. The cinch, secured to the right D-ring with a strap leather latigo, draped back of Marlboro's elbow. Bill slowly extended a wire hook through the slats and under the paint's belly, deftly catching the dangling cinch ring. As Marlboro rolled his eyes and lashed out a hind foot, Smith drew the cinch under the belly toward him. He threaded the left latigo through the cinch ring from behind and pulled the strap back up and over the D-ring. Marlboro backed against the end gate, the skin of his shoulders twitching. Smith repeated the latigo loop, lacing the strap back through the cinch ring and over the D-ring. He then tucked the latigo tail below the D-ring, threading it from front to back, just inside the strap of his last upward pass. A tug upward and the leather tail was pinched between the D-ring and the strap.

Joe Alexander continued making ready for the fray. He jammed on his scuffed boots, their soft leather set in the comfortable familiarity that comes with wear. One spur, then the other was grasped by the shank and anchored to the heel, first by a twist of baling wire around the front of the boot heel and finally by a wide strap over the arch, buckled on the outside. Separate leather straps buckled about the ankles would keep his boots from pulling off—a precaution learned after an overzealous spurring lick had left him half-barefooted at a Phoenix rodeo early in his career.

Joe's spurs were handmade. Blunt star-shaped rowels—larger than generally used by the bareback fraternity—rolled on large centerholes at the tips of two-inch shanks canted a dozen degrees inward. The combination was ideal, giving the champion maximum contact and drag in his spurring lick.

Joe shook out his brown batwing chaps and hitched the belt buckle in front. The white fringe barely swept the ground as he

18

fastened the leg straps above the back of each knee. The chaps had been crafted by Tim Bath, a teammate when Joe was on the University of Wyoming rodeo team. Made of lightweight leather, they flapped wildly from the knee with each spurring lick.

Tucking the rosin-stained glove in the front of his chap belt, Joe turned to face the adversary that had dominated his thoughts from the instant he had seen the draw. A thousand times he had imagined the gate cracking open; a thousand times he had spurred that horse through each agonizing jump; a thousand times he had conquered Marlboro in his mind. Joe's pulse was fast; the adrenalin was flowing. Like Marlboro, he was on an emotional high.

Out in the arena, the dignitaries in the grand entry were being introduced. Buster Ivory peered over his glasses at the riders down the line of chutes, hollered "Pull 'em down, boys," then climbed to the backside of chute number one and grasped the flank strap of the first bronc. Joe and Cody Bill stood above Marlboro, straw hats held over their hearts as the national anthem echoed through the grandstands and announcer Chuck Parkison offered the cowboys' invocation. Marlboro shifted with tense anticipation and hammered the back of the chute with his heels.

While Chuck Parkison turned the packed crowd's attention to the first horse and rider of the day, Joe lowered himself into the chute, and planted his feet on the chute slats on either side of the fidgeting paint horse. Carefully keeping his toes turned inward to avoid touching Marlboro's sides with his spurs, he bent forward and grasped the ends of the rigging body. As Bill Smith loosened the left latigo, Joe slowly pushed the rigging forward, prying the ends outward at the front to fit the body as closely forward on the withers as possible. Marlboro was deep through the heart and heavily muscled, infamous for the power he transmitted to the rider's arm. The forward position helped.

Marlboro now was pacing in the narrow confines of the chute,

Joe Alexander on Marlboro, Cheyenne 1974. *Photo by Al Long*

wild in his anticipation. When Bill lifted on the latigo to tighten the cinch, the horse exploded, lunging forward and leaning out over the gate, striking high in the air. The horse fell back and Joe scrambled over the backside of the chute, thankful for the purchase his boots had on the wooden slats.

Again Joe straddled the horse in the chute and slowly, with steady pressure, forced the rigging body forward on the withers. Cody Bill pulled the latigo snug, but didn't "bail" it into him. was tightened only when the action turned to the horse and rider immediately before him. If a bronc, especially the temperamental Marlboro, stood too long with a tightened cinch, his perfor-

mance would suffer. As the judges scored the ride in the arena, Bill handed Joe the trailing tail of the left latigo. Joe brought the excess strap over the withers in front of the rigging, threaded it through the right D-ring, back over the horse, and tucked it under the left D-ring.

The rider in the arena was on the ground. The pickup men were hazing the horse through the gate. Standing over Marlboro, Joe pulled on his long goatskin riding glove. The sticky rosin crackled as he worked each finger deep into the glove. One, two, three, four times he wrapped the leather thong around his gloved wrist, then pulled the knot snug with his teeth and free hand.

21

Bill Smith stood at Marlboro's head, one hand on the halter, the other tugging at the mane of the shifting, pacing bronc. Buster Ivory stood behind the rider, the flank strap in both hands.

Judges Larry Collins and Jim Mihalek moved to either side of the gate. In yellow slickers and four-buckle overshoes, their score sheets tucked in metal clipboards, they were prepared for the annual Cheyenne monsoon. But for now the rain had stopped. Mihalek eyed the chestnut paint. Six times he had tried the horse; six times he had bucked off. The gate men stood by, watching Joe's face.

Joe pulled down his straw hat, tucked each chap back and crouched down on Marlboro's back for the first time, his feet still on the boards beside the horse's shoulders. Slowly he worked his gloved hand under the rawhide handhold, until it was firmly in his grip. He eased his seat up against his hand. Then, with his free hand he slapped his face. He was awake, he was here, he was now, he was ready.

Joe nodded his head.

The latch cracked with a loud report. The timer's thumb stabbed the stopwatch in her palm. The gate popped open to a kaleidoscope of action. Buster Ivory's arms pumped to his chest, drawing the flank strap whirring through the cinch rings, gripping ticklish flanks. Marlboro's powerful legs bunched and pushed off in a mighty leap, high and arching outward, drawing his head up and away from Bill Smith's fanning hands. Joe Alexander's legs shot forward, toes turned outward, spurred heels driving for a purchase on round, hard shoulders. Gripping. Gathering the horse under him. Arm muscles strained, pulling, squeezing to prevent the rigging from flying away with the Pegasus rising beneath him. Taut neck muscles fought to keep the tremendous force from slopping his head back like a Raggedy Andy doll. Joe's free arm traced a long arc over his head, carrying his torso back, into line with the power thrust of the horse that now was dropping, his front end plummeting to the earth. Joe's left leg was reaching for the horse as it fell away to the right. Groin tendons stretched. Dull rowels gripped the elusive shoulders.

Then came the bone-grinding jar. Marlboro's front feet were driven deep beneath the muddy surface of the soil. A puff of dust rose. Heels snapped skyward, twisting to the left. Shock waves spiraled down Joe's arched spine.

Larry Collins and Jim Mihalek leaned forward, peering intently, to see Joe's feet, toes at right angles, heels clutching the chestnut shoulders. The first crucial test was passed; Joe Alexander had marked the horse. The timer's watch showed one second.

Instinctively, every sinew from Joe's buttocks to the arches of his feet contracted against the explosive expanding impact from Marlboro's shoulders. The bronc's hind feet snapped forward under him, futilely striking at the irritating flank cinch before driving solidly to footing beneath the muddy arena surface. With tremendous force he again lunged skyward. Joe tucked in his arm and pulled, as the jerk snatched at the very roots of his arm. His chest expanded, tense. His stomach was taut.

Joe's knees flexed at the bronc's upward drive. His thighs jerked upward, applying resistance to the large, dull spur rowels rolling through the hair up Marlboro's neck. His free arm swept forward. All motion was concerted, resisting the forces wrenching the rigging away from his seat; the handhold from his grasp.

At the zenith of his drive, Marlboro rolled in an arc to the right. His front end began to drop away, his hips ever rising. Joe's free arm again pumped his upper body back, in expectation of the shock of impact. Knees still bent, his thighs simultaneously drove his spurs downward to grasp a purchase on Marlboro's shoulders (Olly, Olly, Oxen Free) before the mighty horse jarred his hooves to the earth.

As he hit, Marlboro flexed his right elbow, fading the shoulder from the tip of Joe's heel. The rigging lurched downward after the elusive shoulder, as if into a well. Then hind hooves shot outward, striking to the left.

Joe's stomach chilled. It felt as though the horse was stumbling. In reflex, he tucked his left leg tightly and pumped the free arm skyward, away from the well.

Mihalek watched the struggle with understanding. He too had felt the sickening stumbling sensation. Six times he had failed to master the ploy. At the other side of the chute Larry Collins missed the move, appreciating instead the rider's timing in concerting his motions with the wild moves of the horse.

In an instant the wily bronc's motion reversed. Hind feet driving to the ground, Marlboro pitched upward sharply to the right. Now Joe was jerked by a tremendous thrust tilting him outside to the left and into his riding arm. Again in reflex, his right spur caught the elusive round shoulder. His free arm swung forward. Knees jerked, thighs lifted, heels resisted the horse slipping upward and away from their grasp.

At the peak of his spurring lick, Joe's spur rowels no longer could help. His arm alone bore the violent force that pushed his torso backward. The handhold bit deeply into his grip, pinching the little finger and heel of his gloved hand.

Marlboro dropped in reentry, spiraling ever to the right. Joe's legs shot downward, driving his heels to a safe purchase on the shoulders. They hit the bottom together. The timer's watch showed two seconds elapsed.

This time Joe was ready for the dip of the right shoulder, the trap of the well. His motions were a ballet of balance in counterpoint to the crafty Marlboro's tricks.

Ever circling to the right, stage center in front of the bucking chutes, Marlboro launched skyward with terrific thrust. Joe's spur rowels would drag upward to his handhold; then his arm would be at the mercy of the snatching power. Only the trip-hammer driving of his knees to regain a spur hold on the broad shoulders could save Joe from having the rawhide torn from his grasp. Only the pumping of his free arm, rocking his torso back at the downward plunge, could keep him from being ejected over Marlboro's head. Only the grip of his spurs could keep the paint horse from ducking from between his legs once he'd dropped the right shoulder.

Where a smaller horse would weaken as the seconds ticked by, Marlboro's power never diminished. Each jump arched high into the air. Each crash to the earth struck with bone-shaking authority. The bronc's heels flashed first high above the rider's head, then ratcheting to the left, in broken cadence. And always the lurch of the shoulder drop; always the magnetic pull of the well.

The thud of hooves, grunts of rushing air, creak of leather, and shouts from the cowboys lining the chutes melded in a single incessant roar inside Joe's head. His neck muscles bulged. His jaw was drawn with the crazy spiraling force. Each movement was magnified, time seemingly in slow motion. Each jarring shock wave traveled the full length of his spine. Each dip and shift of the horse whiplashed through his body. Each power thrust whirring between his heels hit the end of his arm in heightened force. Ever he was charging, driving, squeezing, dragging, pulling, and driving once again. Aggressively attacking. Fighting to keep his heels close to the horse, knowing if his body crossed against the power thrust, if his legs were forced to spraddle, gapping over his head, he would be blown away, torn from his weakening grasp.

The blaring horn rasped through the rolling fog of dizziness. It was over. Joe lurched forward, grabbing the front of his rigging with his free hand, squeezing the cinch with his legs, waggling his gloved hand free from the rosined handhold. A pickup man rushed in close on his left, grabbing the belt of his chaps from behind, lifting him as his own gloved hand encircled the savior's waist. Joe kicked his legs high, clear of Marlboro's treacherous heels, as the other pickup man thundered past on the right, tripping the release on the flank strap. Joe dropped to the ground, staggering with the dizziness in his head, clutching his aching arm to his chest.

The judges turned in their score sheets. Collins marked Marlboro a 20. To Joe he awarded a 23. Larry Collins fully appreciated the control with which Joe Alexander rode. Jim Mihalek scored Marlboro a 25, the ultimate. He knew the bronc's array of tricks and he had not missed their dazzling display. With admiration he judged Joe equal to the horse. The lights on the Winston scoreboard flashed out the verdict. Joe Alexander had scored a 93, the highest mark in bareback riding history.

Joe sighed, a warmth seeping through the tiredness. He also had just won the 1974 Cheyenne Frontier Days, the Daddy Of 'Em All.

He was ready to head on down the road, to the next rodeo.

Roy Cooper's Inner Game

Roy Cooper is perhaps the greatest calf roper that rodeo has seen, and the remarkable footnote to his string of calf-roping championships is that there was a time in 1979 when the sages of the toprail would have predicted that the fast roping Roy would never again win a world championship, or even rope in competition.

In June 1979 Roy Cooper was among the leaders in the calf roping, standing third with $19,223, behind leader Tom Ferguson and John Rothwell of Hyannis, Nebraska, then in second slot. Between rodeos, Cooper was at Ernie Taylor's arena at Hugo, Oklahoma, practicing to keep his skills honed to a razor's edge. "I had one more calf to run," he told Bill Crawford of the PRCA. "I made the run and caught the calf and I was hanging out there on the dismount and my rope was too stiff. A coil flopped up and around my wrist. I knew what had happened and tried to shuck the coil off but there was nothing I could do. The calf came to the end of the rope and my wrist was shattered by the impact. I wish it had broken my arm in three places. That would be a lot easier to deal with."

Cooper was rushed into Hugo for X-rays, and on to Paris,

Texas. Swelling was tremendous, and the pain nearly unbearable. Cooper was in danger of losing the hand. Referred first to Dr. Evans of the Dallas Cowboys, and finally to Dr. Peter Carter, also of Dallas, "the greatest hand surgeon in the world," Cooper underwent extensive surgery to repair the shattered bones with steel pins and a steel screw where the large forearm bone, the ulna, was reattached.

For a time Cooper was held in suspense as to the success of the operation. "The whole thing depends upon whether or not unrestricted blood circulation is, or can be, restored to my wrist," he explained to Crawford. For weeks Cooper could only look hopelessly at his fingers projecting beyond the plaster cast. But a spirit deep inside him refused to give up. Roy was determined, somehow, to rope again.

Other operations followed, to repair the damage to muscle, tendon, nerve, and bone. Then came the agonizing therapy. With religious fervor, he exercised the stiff and swollen hand, pushing himself to the limit, fighting back the pain.

Within two months Roy Cooper was back in the practice arena. First he roped with his left arm. If that was what it took, he would relearn all that he had put together over his twenty-three years. But all the while he continued exercising his right hand and wrist. As pain and swelling subsided, therapy loosened the stiff joint, stretching ligaments despite the pin that would remain for the rest of his life.

By September he was roping in competition, and placing. Slowly his earnings increased: $20,203 reported in the standings for September 19, with a tenuous hold on ninth place. By September 24, he had slipped to eleventh place, but his earnings rose to $20,688. On October 8, he was back to tenth, with $23,249. By the October 22 he dropped back to twelfth in the pre-Finals run, but his earnings continued to rise, to $23,586. Going into

Roy Cooper, NFR 1979. *Photo by James Fain, courtesy* World of Rodeo.

the National Finals, Roy's earnings stood at $23,974, good enough to stave off the competition for twelfth berth. Out of action from June until September, through the most lucrative months of the rodeo season, Roy Cooper still was able to make it to the Finals, and add an additional $3,771 during his comeback from the wrist injury.

That he made it to the 1979 National Finals is in itself a dramatic success story of courage and determination, but the truly amazing miracle came during the Finals. When the dust settled after the final performance at the new Myriad facility in downtown Oklahoma City, just five months after doctors had warned him that he might never rope again, Roy Cooper won the NFR calf roping, 107.9 seconds on ten head.

He finished the 1979 season with $38,974, in seventh position.

To visit with Roy Cooper is to know that it could have been no other way. There is a fierce determination beneath his easy grin; it is a toughness that has come to be synonymous with "cowboy."

There is also a fascinating story behind the rigor of self-discipline that the young champion can tell. He calls it his inner game. And it can be expressed in one word: breathing.

"Think about it," Cooper explained. "You are more relaxed at the outstroke of your breath. Pete Gay and I were talking about it behind the chutes. If you hold your breath, you tense up. Like in bull riding, when you nod for the gate when you are holding your breath, you have no energy at all. You tighten up and have no power. Breathing lets the tension out. You relax, your reflexes and reactions are uninhibited.

"Watch a boxing match. Ali jabs with the outstroke of his breath. You can hear him: Oooff. That's him hitting, not the reaction of the man being hit."

"When I'm up in calf roping, I approach the box, concentrating on nothing but my breathing. I force myself to breathe evenly and deeply in a carefully metered rhythm. I force all other thoughts out of my head. I become more relaxed, and my body reacts best."

To illustrate Roy Cooper's inner game in operation, let's take a typical run in competition. Roy rides into the roping box and turns his horse around. The world outside—the flurry of the rodeo, and the time he has to beat in the calf-roping contest—is beyond his consciousness. His thoughts are on his breathing: carefully metered, relaxed breathing. By turning his thoughts inward he contains his emotions, controls his tensions. A confidence pervades his being.

Roy already knows how he wants to set behind the barrier in

the roping box; knows how he will score the calf, begin his pursuit; when he will make his throw. He knows how the rope will curl above the calf's neck, how he will handle his all-important slack; make his run to the calf with planned steps, flank the animal to the ground; make his tie, his three wraps, and a half-hitch "hooey."

Roy knows because, although he is only twenty-four, he has made every move a thousand times before. It isn't the age that seasons the roper, it is the miles of rope that have passed through his hands. It is throwing the loop consistently, like Toots Mansfield and Dean Oliver. Handling his slack in the manner of Don McLaughlin. Tying calves in cold winter barns since he was eight years old. Practicing. Learning the right way. Applying Olin Young's first wrap, Don McLaughlin's second wrap, Ronnye Sewalt's hooey. Just like his dad Tuffy Cooper had shown him.

Each run, each calf, is different, requiring a different combination of moves. But Roy Cooper knows exactly how he will make this run. By following his prescription for action, without flaw.

And by breathing: his inner game.

His saddle is of his own design, crafted by saddlemaker Billy Cook of Greenville, Texas. The 13½-inch swells give good thigh grip; the laid back cantle gives ample clearance for Roy's flying dismounts. His feet find solid support in the deep stirrups, critical support for the roper who makes his throws from a standing position, leaning forward to the right, out over his work.

A 6½-foot pigging string of small, medium-hard twist nylon is carried in his teeth with a seven-inch noose ready formed. A spare is tucked in easy reach, under the right side of his belt. Roy threads the braided rein loop in over the ring finger of his left hand. The excess rein is laid back forward, down over the top of his little finger. His hand is free to hold the coils of his 93-strand, medium-hard twist 7/16-inch untreated sisal rope.

Roy carries a small loop in the 26-foot rope under his right arm. To keep the loop open, and to control the dip in roping, the honda lays a quarter circle forward from his right-hand grip on the loop and spoke of slack leading to the coils in his left hand.

From his left hand, Roy's rope passes through a rope loop around the base of the rope horse's neck to its attachment with a plaited collar to the saddle horn. Running the rope from the horn out through the neck loop keeps the roping horse in a straight line, facing the calf after a catch has been made.

Roy's spare rope is coiled and attached with twine to a metal ring stapled to the right front of his saddle fork. Its ready-built loop is tucked out of the way forward under the saddle breast collar. Like the rope in Roy's hand, the free end passes through a special control loop before attaching on the saddle horn below the tie of his first loop.

A jerkline, too, is attached to the left side of the bridle. Passing over a pully on the left saddle swell, the loose end is tucked in convolutions under the left side of Roy's belt. As he runs to the calf this line will pull free, giving the horse a tug to remind him to stop and hold back in a straight line against the calf on the other end of the rope.

Roy also has a tie-down strap attached from the bridle to the front of the sturdy breast collar. Eliminating problems of erratic roping horse behavior is the name of the equipment game, easing the task of performing the flawless run, making it uncomfortable to err.

Roy quarters the horse in the roping box on a diagonal toward the calf as the barrier is secured. A light handle on the rein keeps the horse under control, standing at attention, waiting for his rider's cue. Roy watches the tail man line out the calf in the chute, laying an imaginary yardstick down the calf's back, picking a reference point on the chute from which to measure the calf's escape.

The calf is ready, shoving his muzzle against the gates, craving the arena's freedom.

Roy waits, timing his breathing rhythm. He nods his head.

The gate man pumps the handle. The gates fly open. The calf is free, running.

Roy watches the inches on his imaginary yardstick slip past his reference point with the escape of the calf. Seven inches. Eight. Nine. Ten.

With a controlled outstroke of his breath, Roy pushes the rein to the horse's neck. Comes upright in his stirrups. Squeezes with his legs. His heels.

The horse lunges at the barrier, hundredths of a second behind the calf's arrival at the score line, at the end of the cord about his neck. The cord jerks taut. Breaks free. Falls to the dirt. The barrier flies through the air, brushed aside by the driving shoulders of the rope horse.

Already Roy's right arm is elevated. Forward. The loop makes its first swing, tilted above the roper's head. The circle grows as he feeds slack line through the rawhide honda burner.

The horse charges down on the fleeing calf. His neck is low, outstretched. Running to the "hole." Nose reaching for the calf's swirling frayed rope of a tail.

Roy's second swing begins his throw. Standing in his stirrups, he leans forward to the right. With the release of his breath, he releases the loop with calm control. He delivers the loop from the palm of his hand, with a commanding twist of his wrist.

The front of the loop dips, scooping under the muzzle of his quarry. The open loop snags against the right side of the animal's neck. The loop's rotation, given impetus by Roy's wrist action, accelerates around in front. Curls upward, high over the left side of the calf's neck, in a picture-book figure-eight curl. The calf is caught.

Roy brakes his horse. Slips his left foot out of the deep stirrup.

Rolls his leg back over the low-set saddle seat. In the same fluid motion he draws in the sisal line. Jerking the slack horizontally, decisively to the right of the path of his horse.

Roy follows the snaking rope with his body. Exiting to the right of the skidding rope horse. Running with precise placement of his feet. Breathing with practiced control. Leaning into his run. Right hand reaching forward. Anticipating cattle. His left elbow hooks over the rope. Left hand sliding over the tight-twisted fibers.

The heavy jerkline draws tight. Tugs back against the bridle bit and nose hobble. Enforces the skidding stop. Then pulls free from under Roy's belt to fall, function fulfilled, behind the sprinting man.

With Roy on the ground in pursuit, the calf hits the end of the line. Not with a terrific jerk, to be upended in a backward somersault, but spun around counterclockwise to face the roper. Descending on the calf, Roy plays the tension on the rope with trained reflex, like a master fly-fisherman. This fish will not get away.

Roy meets the calf as his horse leans back against the rope, coming out of his four-footed slide. Roy's left hand catches the calf at the honda of his rope. His extended right arm reaches over the butterball flanks, his fist gripping a full hand of loose hide. He is square with the left side of his 300-pound adversary. On the outstroke of his breath his knees bend in reflex. Crouching deep. Scooping under. Upending the animal sideways into his lap.

Roy's left hand reaches out, his fingers close around the calf's upper right foreleg at the peak of his lift. Rolling the calf onto the low workbench of his thighs, Roy releases his flank grip. His right hand sweeps the pigging string out of his mouth. Unerringly he catches the captured foreleg in his pigging string loop. On the outstroke of his breath.

Tension is gone. His muscles react smoothly, in reflex motions fine-tuned from endless practice.

The calf still is off the ground. Roy's right arm sweeps back toward the calf's hind legs, drawing the pigging string taut, tightening the noose about the captured foreleg. The tail of the string slips from his fingers, falling to the ground, exactly in the same position it has always fallen a thousand times before.

The horse holds tension on the rope, leaning back, all four feet on the ground, working the rope, ears forward, watching the action on the other end of the line.

The calf slides onto the ground, facing away from Roy's knees. Once more breathing out, Roy snags the calf's lower, left hind leg from behind, scooping it forward in the valley between his thumb and forefinger. The upper leg is gathered, catching against his forearm as his same right hand closes around the string lying on the ground exactly where he knew it would be.

Continuing the forward sweep of his right arm, Roy draws the hind legs ahead to cross over the top of the foreleg caught in the pigging string noose. Crouching low, Roy swings his right leg around behind the calf, then carries it forward, catching the hind legs between the hip and hock, holding them forward. Steady. Low to the ground. Avoiding a panic, a kick to regain equilibrium lost.

With the pigging string still in his right hand, half of Roy's first wrap already is completed.

With controlled motion he continues the forward sweep. Rolling his hand over the top of the three gathered legs. Around beneath. Completing the first wrap.

His hand describes a tight circle around his wrap. Feeding string through his fingers with just the right tension. His wrist barely clears the projecting hooves. His motion is fluid, efficient, calculated, controlled.

Like his metered breathing. Roy Cooper is fast, not hurried.

At the end of his second turn around the three legs, Roy holds his left hand out above the tied limbs, palm up. The circle of his wrap lays the string across his open hand. The forward motion of his right hand gathers the two hind legs in the third wrap. Then he short-cuts the wrap. Around the jutting hind hooves, excluding the front hoof which projects rearward.

With the fingers of his left hand, Roy catches the string drawn across the valley between the calf's hind legs and front hoof. His fingers close around the middle of the string. Draws it through, under the previous wrap over his left hand.

An upward jerk. The "hooey" half-hitch is complete. Tight. Roy's hands continue in smooth motion upward. Signaling completion of the tie.

Roy's breathing, his unhurried inner game, is on the in stroke.

The World in
Four-Tenths of a Second

Leo Camarillo was the World Champion All-Around Cowboy of 1975.

Tom Ferguson was the World Champion All-Around Cowboy of 1975.

Leo Camarillo and Tom Ferguson were the World Champion All-Around Cowboys of 1975.

In "rodeo's finest hour," the 1975 National Finals Rodeo, before a nationwide television audience, Leo Camarillo and Tom Ferguson were weighed in the balances of the Professional Rodeo Cowboy's Association, and the antiquated balances were found wanting. The awarding of points toward the all-around cowboy championship touched off a blazing bonfire of discontent that threatened to send organized rodeo up in smoke. The cross fire of accusation and recrimination, audit and re-audit, shocked to attention the staid rodeo establishment—complacent in its cultivated image of easygoing independence and rugged individualism.

And from the heat of controversy the PRCA was reborn, like the legendary Phoenix rising from its own ashes, to belatedly join the computerized twentieth century, to operate as a vital, sophisticated business organization instead of a friendly behind-the-chutes game of craps.

Tom Ferguson was alone at the top during the previous year, claiming the all-around title by a $32,000 margin over his closest competitor, Leo Camarillo. However, Tom got off to a slow start in 1975, picking up only chicken feed at the indoor shows early in the season. Leo, in contrast, jumped out to a solid lead. The title see-sawed back and forth through a season involving 575 sanctioned rodeos and over $6 million in prize monies. As it came down to the wire it was evident that the World All-Around Championship would be decided at the National Finals.

Three times before the Finals, Tom Ferguson had telephoned the PRCA office. Three times he had asked if their records had been audited, if their totals were correct. Three times the PRCA had assured him that their figures were in order.

Leo Camarillo qualified for the Finals in the team roping only, $2,266 ahead of Tom—no comfortable margin considering that Tom had made it both in calf roping and steer wrestling. At a distant third, six-time all-around champion Larry Mahan had an outside shot at overhauling Camarillo, qualifying in the bareback and saddle bronc riding events.

Because half of his earnings would go to his header, H. P. Evetts, the most Leo could make by winning a go-round would be $469.49; his share of a first in the average payoff would be $1,021.13. Tom and Larry each could earn $892.82 with a go-round win, $1,941.88 by taking the average in a single event. On paper, the all-around title was up for grabs.

As the Finals progressed, consistency became the watchword for Tom Ferguson. At the close of the eighth go-round on Friday night, Larry Mahan was out of the average in bareback contention, having goose-egged opening night on Walt Alsbaugh's Spark Plug. In the saddle bronc riding he had managed a two-thirds split, and a first, with an 82 score on Alsbaugh's Hi-Dive.

Tom Ferguson and Peanuts, C. R. Jones hazing. *Photo by Dave Allen*

Camarillo, despite two firsts and a one-two split, was having dismal success in the team roping average race. The first night it took he and Evetts three loops, and a five-second penalty for a single-heel catch. Their time was a frustrating 36.8 seconds.

Ferguson had gathered some $1,200 in the calf roping and was sitting in third place for the average. His steer wrestling winnings from a third placing in the opening go-round added nearly $450, and his total time put him in seventh position in that event. By Saturday, with two go-rounds and the average yet to be decided, Leo Camarillo's lead had dropped to $1,941.72, within Ferguson's reach.

From the time he could catch the house cat with a pigging string and shinny up a rope tied to the saddle horn to bull-dog goats and a recalcitrant burro from the back of his Shetland pony, jackpotting for marbles with his older brother Larry, all Tom Ferguson ever wanted to do in life was rodeo: "I always planned to go down the road. All my life, all I ever wanted to be was a professional cowboy."

Ira Ferguson, the boys' dad, had rodeoed seriously in all the events after moving his Oklahoma family to San Martin, California, when Tom was three. The steady stream of rodeo greats coming to the Fergusons' practice arena—Ira started 1973 Steer Wrestling Champion Bob Marshall bulldogging—gave the boys all the encouragement they needed. During his freshman year in college, the 5-foot, 11-inch, 175-pound Tom qualified for the Cal Poly rodeo team and captured reserve champion steer wrestling honors in the National Intercollegiate Rodeo Association. In his junior year, 1972, he missed the national NIRA calf roping championship by three points.

He also gathered his first prize at a major PRCA show in 1972: a rope can. But from this small beginning, he jumped out the next year to win $45,447 on the professional circuit, second only to the indefatigable Larry Mahan. Tom also was runner-up in the NIRA national all-around standings.

When the marbles were up, Tom Ferguson played to win.

Tom's professional steer wrestling wins mostly were from the back of C. R. Jones's famed 'dogging horse Peanuts. The eleven-year-old red sorrel gelding with the white star on his forehead was the picture of quarter horse conformation. He stood 14 hands at 1,150 pounds, solid as a rock with heavy bones and well-balanced muscling. His speed was phenomenal. As a coming two-year-old, under the famed Jackie Robinson, he had won nine of eleven starts on the highly competitive Los Alamitos track. His sire Breeze Bars was a racing recordholder; his dam Camelot's Broom, a California state barrel-racing champion.

Peanuts was trained by Jones, first as a hazing horse for his bay, Big Print: "the human smartest horse I ever rode in my life. He can read a man's feelings."

After the first year, when Peanuts had learned to "score" cattle, waiting for the rider's cue before breaking from the box, C. R. switched the animals' roles. It was a profitable combination. Peanuts developed a reputation around the rodeo circuit for being a solid horse to ride. He would park himself to stand flatfooted in the box until his rider gave the signal, regardless of the noise about him or the movements of the steer. And he could catch cattle, consistently "rating" them, adjusting his speed to that of a steer until the dogger made his move—holding steady under the sudden shift in weight; then accelerating, really turning it on, to carry the dogger's feet ahead of the action. Although he didn't depart with a lead to the left like most doggers desire, to Tom Ferguson "there never was a 'dogging horse other than Peanuts."

The veteran Big Print, too, carried out his role precisely with his "human sense," carrying C. R. to the steer in exact synchronization with Peanuts. Big Print didn't "cheat" steers by arriving early to muscle them into position. He didn't have to. They were a perfectly matched team.

On Saturday night before the performance, C. R. Jones fed each horse half of his daily two-gallon ration of crimped oats and sweet feed. C. R. carefully metered the animals' nutrition to their physical exertion. He kept them supplied with 707-vitamin pellets and once each week he gave them intravenous shots of B_{12}, liver, and iron. Before the rodeo he wrapped Peanuts' front legs with cold water wraps. Like a racehorse, the front legs of a dogging horse took a tremendous pounding. The horse

41

has been said to be 75 percent of a good bulldogging run, and C. R. Jones saw to it that his would be up to the demand.

Jones was forty-seven. He himself had qualified for the National Finals, his first since 1964, when the Finals had been held in Los Angeles. C. R. was not up tonight, though. He'd drawn no times since injuring his knee in the fourth go-round, and he finally checked it in after Friday's attempt, hurting too badly to continue. Tonight he was concentrating solely on his dogging team and what he had to do as a hazer for the four riders who were mounted on Peanuts: the Ferguson boys, Darrel Sewell, and Frank Shepperson, leader in the year's steer wrestling standings.

The first fans were filing into the plush Jim Norick Arena at the Oklahoma State Fair Grounds on Oklahoma City's west side. C. R. put a hackamore headstall with woven reins on his prize dogging horse. A blanket, pad and a spur-tracked old Veach bulldogging saddle were placed on Peanuts's back. Jones drew the front cinch snug and loosely fastened the back cinch to hang straight down, moored to the front girth with a hobble. The right stirrup too was hobbled to the front cinch, to keep it from flopping out of control during a steer wrestling run. C. R. hooked up the breast collar, used to keep the saddle from slipping back from Peanuts's tremendous acceleration. Jones didn't use the customary tie-down. With the well-schooled Peanuts, none was needed. Saddling Big Print with a regular stock saddle, he led the sorrel into the arena for a brisk ten-minute workout, getting his legs limbered, his breathing regulated.

The steer wrestling was the second event on the program. The time to shoot for was quickly established by the jovial 6-foot-6-inch giant Fred Larsen. Out of contention for the average with a 46.8 second run in the eighth go-round the previous evening, Fred was strictly out for go-round money. In go-for-broke recklessness he bedded his steer in a sizzling 3.9 seconds.

Three runs later Bob Marshall equaled the phenomenal clocking.

Larry Ferguson had trouble in shaping his steer and the clock rolled up 22.8 seconds before his animal was laid over to take the judge's flag. By brother Tom's turn, the time to beat still was 3.9, and Larry's lead over Tom for sixth place and $334.81 in the average had dwindled considerably.

The pressure was intense, electric in the air. Tom Ferguson, Leo Camarillo, each spectator in Jim Norick Arena, and every viewer glued to television sets across the nation knew it was do or die. Tom Ferguson had to have those marbles.

Tom had drawn the best of the cattle. In four of the previous go-rounds the steer wrestling had been won on the red Mexican-cross steer with the white face. Tom knew he would break solid from the gate, run with moderate speed in a straight line, and so far had shown no tendency to "set up" or skid to a halt at the dogger's approach from behind.

Tom shortened both stirrups to equal length—most doggers ride a right stirrup set slightly longer than the left—tightened the cinch, and mounted the sorrel. He breathed deeply, calming the butterflies within his chest. Doubling the rein in his right hand he inserted his little finger between the two strands, laying the excess over the top of his hand. The right rein he held slightly shorter, for better control in his plunge.

Warmed from exertion Peanuts was ready to work under Tom's familiar hand. They approached the left-hand box, circled to face the red steer. At the same instant C. R. wheeled Big Print in mirror image within the opposite compartment.

The tail man slipped the Hallettsville barrier cord around the steer's neck, then closed the neck loop with a tie of twine. Chute helpers stretched the loose cord end across the front of Tom's box. Peanuts parked himself, flatfooted, his rump in the far corner of the box, his muscles bunched, coiled springs, his eye never wavering from the quarry.

The gate man, sitting above the steer chute, rattled the batwing end gates, tantalizing the animal within. The tail man maneuvered the steer into position. Larry Ferguson stood in the near corner, ready to assist.

Tom held light pressure on the rein, his left hand grasping the saddle horn, his right leg bent slightly at the knee. He watched the steer, saw it eye the light of freedom through the crack ahead. C. R. called to his dogger. He was at ready. It was time to call for cattle.

Tom nodded his head. His eye shifted to the gate, sighting across the taut barrier. The gate man pumped the handle, releasing the anxious animal. Still, Peanuts stood in check. Tom gauged the white-faced steer's flight past the barrier pin. His head. His neck. Shoulders. Back. Hip.

Tom pushed the rein forward. Pulled on the saddle horn. Stood in the stirrups. Peanuts lunged on cue, arriving at the barrier at the slightest instant after his prey reached the score line twelve feet beyond the open gate. The steer hit the end of the neck rope headlong, tripping the barrier free, breaking the flimsy tie twine. Peanuts brushed aside the flying barrier cord.

The sorrel horse immediately closed the distance to the fleeing steer. Big Print arrived instantaneously on the right. Tom dropped the rein. Leaned out in pursuit. Stood knee bent in the right stirrup. Suspended from his left handgrip. Even with the steer's tail. His hip. Tom released the saddle horn. Diving over the steer.

His right arm swooped over the animal's back, his neck. Scooped the right horn into the crook of his elbow. Gathered the steer's head against his ribs.

Tom's left hand shot downward. His palm slammed against the left horn. At its polished tip.

His left leg slid across the saddle. Toes turned up. The spur rowel rolling. Over the scarred saddle seat.

Peanuts poured on the speed, gaskin muscles pulsing in drive, at twenty, twenty-five miles per hour. His ears were laid back, his neck outstretched. Tom hung, suspended in air, between the steer's curly head and his right foot in the hobbled stirrup.

The dogger's feet were carried forward with the sorrel's acceleration. Knees flexed, he recovered body control. Dug the balls of his feet into the damp arena loam. Held his body low, off the ground. Drew his left leg back, turning his foot, dragging it sideways. His right leg, his rudder, paralleled the racing steer. His body eased outward—45, 50, 70 degrees away from their path.

With mighty exertion, Tom shoved the left horn down. Hauled upward against the right horn in the bend of his arm. Like a boxer letting fly a right cross. In close. Keeping the head against his body. Into his lap. Steady. Capturing the animal's sense of balance.

Tom's right leg brought forward motion to a stop. From his deep body position, he pushed with his left leg. Shoved his right hip into the steer's neck and shoulder. Tipping the animal over his hip. Off its front legs, its balance completely in his control.

Releasing his grip on the left horn, Tom rolled to the sides of his feet. Twisted his torso, clockwise. Hooked the animal's muzzle deep within the crook of his left arm. Hugging the horned head close. Allowing no bobbing, no wasted motion.

Now he was facing down the steer's spine. He braced the side of his left foot into the ground. Strained upward on his arms. Rolling the animal's head about the fulcrum of his right hip. Pulling the nose into his face.

The red steer's rear quarters rose in the air. Helpless against the force of their own momentum.

Tom arched his back. Pushed with his legs. Pulled with his arms. Reaching the pressure point. Falling backward. Cattle and man. Dropping to the earth.

The animal rolled onto his back, four feet jutting helpless in the air. Conquered.

The field judge dropped his flag with a snap.

C. R. Jones turned in his saddle. The action was over. The arena clock read 3.5 seconds.

Tom twisted over, anxiously searching the front of the chutes for the barrier judge. He was clean. He had not broken the barrier. The time, 3.5 seconds, would stand.

Tom Ferguson had beaten his competition by four-tenths of second. This go-round, these marbles, were his.

Heads wagged, collecting, comprehending what eyes had taken in; 3.5 seconds: the quickest clocking in the entire eleven-year history of the National Finals Rodeo.

It also was the last go-round money that Tom, or any of the three all-around contenders, would take home from the National Finals. In the team roping Leo Camarillo and H. P. Evetts jumped out in an all-or-none effort. Evetts—the header who throws one of the longest ropes in the business—snaked out his loop to gather in an illegal head catch. They were flagged a no-time. In dejection Leo watched the steer exit through the catch pen gate, with Evetts's tangled rope and hopes for the average dragging along behind in the Oklahoma dirt.

Larry Mahan had drawn Reg Kesler's Buckskin Billy in the saddle bronc riding. Three jumps into the arena the horse stumbled, falling to his knees. Mahan pitched out his rein, catapulting over the "dashboard," under the scrambling hooves. He staggered to his feet, clutching his right arm to his side, the elbow dislocated. His all-around hopes shattered in flashing neon pain.

In the calf roping, world leader Jeff Copenhaver was forced to use two ropes, dropping out of average contention. Tom Ferguson tied his calf in 11.6 seconds, a solid run with no mistakes. Too slow for the Saturday purse, but keeping him alive in the average.

At the end of the evening Tom Ferguson was $892.81 closer to the All-Around Championship of the World.

The final performance on Sunday, December 15, 1975, was ushered in with an icy wind out of the north. Gust by twenty-five mile per hour gust, the damp chill penetrated each animal and man to the bone. The leaden sky framed Jim Norick Arena in a bleak canvas for the desperate drama painted that afternoon.

Gingerly cradling his throbbing arm, Larry Mahan provided commentary for the television audience. In the first event of the final day Joe Alexander, displaying his prowess with commanding control, claimed the bareback riding diadem aboard Beutler Brothers and Cervi's Little Dan.

Next came the steer wrestling. Larry Ferguson fell victim to fickle fate, drawing the same obstreperous steer that had knocked Darrel Sewell and Casper Schaefer, in turn, out of the average. Larry "cowboyed up," putting out his best effort, but it took two runs and nearly thirty-eight seconds to halt the pulsing numbers lighting up the electronic arena clock.

Then it was Tom Ferguson's turn. He would need 3.7 seconds to again better the juggernaut Fred Larsen and win the go-round, 4.4 seconds to place. But only 20.9 to pull ahead of brother Larry for fourth money in the average.

Tom bedded down his ox in 4.9. He had closed the gap to $714.10.

In the team roping, Leo Camarillo and H. P. Evetts again drew a no-time. Leo's heel loop fell empty to the ground. Camarillo slumped in the saddle. He knew he was at the mercy of Tom Ferguson. The calf roping was yet to come.

Ferguson was the next to last man out. He would need a 15.8 to cinch a fourth place in the average, to surpass Leo Camarillo, to claim the all-around title.

It was no time for heroics. Just a smooth run. With no mistakes.

Tom held back at the barrier, watching it fall. Then rising in the stirrups, hot in pursuit. His horse fell in behind the calf, "rating" the animal's speed precisely, setting up the perfect toss. Tom's wrist rolled. He released the loop. Unerringly it settled over the fleeing calf's head. The roper's arm jerked upward. Hauling in the slack. Whirring the rope through the honda. Tightening the noose. Tom was off his horse. Running.

The calf hit the end of the rope. And fell backward. Stunned.

Tom strained to lift the limp animal to its feet. Struggling against three hundred pounds of inertia. The calf would not budge.

Second by agonizing second the arena clock flashed its damning message to the scene of pathos below.

With sheer determination Tom righted the inert veal against his knees. To satisfy the rule book. And the field judge's critical eye. He flopped the animal on its side. Scooped up three flailing legs. Tied the pigging string: "Three wraps and a hooey."

Tom Ferguson stepped back. Raised his arms in finis. In frustration.

The mockery of the clock stopped at 24.4 seconds.

In the officials' booth fingers manipulated keyboards. Calculators signaled answers. Tom Ferguson had finished the calf roping with a 157.9 second total. Fifth place, $602.65. Just $111.45 short. Short of the goal that had relentlessly driven him on down a hundred thousand miles of road to a hundred rodeos in a hundred cities and towns.

Leo Camarillo was declared the World Champion All-Around Cowboy of 1975. With a "Ya hoo" hoarse with pent-up emotion, he pitched his black hat spiraling high in the air. To Larry Mahan and a nation of television viewers he murmured in reverent Catholic benediction, "God is a team roping fan."

Ira and Maxine Ferguson had kept close account of the earnings of their two rodeoing sons. Their tallies did not jive with those of the PRCA. As had Tom, Ira requested an audit of point totals long before the National Finals Rodeo had convened in Oklahoma City. When Tom returned to the family ranch just north of Miami, Oklahoma, his parents urged him to follow through on their concerns. If it was possible that the PRCA staff had credited the earnings of one Ferguson to the account of another, what about the totals of the Camarillo brothers, Leo and Jerold, and their cousin Reg? The hand-posting process was subject to myriad human errors.

During the annual PRCA convention in January 1976 Tom dropped by the main office up the hill behind Denver's Bronco Stadium, just off I-25. Within twenty minutes of his arrival Tom located a major error in the year's totals. He dug deeper.

Tom voiced his concerns to the PRCA Board of Directors.

He was placed on the agenda for the board meeting in San Antonio in February. Except when Tom and his lawyer arrived, not enough board members showed to make a quorum. Six hours later the last necessary director arrived. Tom presented his evidence. His final, corrected totals revealed he had earned $245 more in 1975 than had Leo Camarillo. He wanted the title that was rightly his: World Champion All-Around Cowboy of 1975.

To Leo Camarillo, victim of the hand-posting errors, it was a nightmare beyond belief. Hadn't he been declared champion? Hadn't the official PRCA totals decided it? Hadn't it been announced to the entire world that he was the World Champion All-Around Cowboy of 1975?

They could not take that away from him. Not now.

Camarillo assured the PRCA Board of Directors that he would sue should they attempt to strip him of the title for which he had worked so hard and had been told by the officials of the PRCA that he had earned.

The board took the grave situation under advisement. They audited their tallies. Leo Camarillo audited the figures. But no matter how it was calculated, Tom Ferguson was right. He had won the most money in 1975.

The PRCA sued the accounting firm initially responsible for the pre-NFR "official" standings audit. But Tom Ferguson still was short the $10,000, the handsome championship buckle, the Scriver bronze statue of Bill Linderman, the awards, recognition, and commercial endorsements that rightfully, legally were his.

Then, in a terse news release, the Professional Rodeo Cowboys of America announced their compromise solution: "Concluding a two-month investigation, the Board of Directors of the PRCA has declared that both Leo Camarillo and Tom Ferguson are the World Champion All-Around Cowboys for 1975 . . . " Each, the Board announced, had earned $50,300 plus.

Both Leo Camarillo and Tom Ferguson were winners. Both were losers. Each, from his own perspective, is bitter about the points awards for 1975. Each was a victim of innacuracies, of ineptitudes, of a system that failed.

The system since has changed. Even as the controversy over the 1975 points awards exploded, the PRCA moved into a mechanized system—pioneered by bullrider Jerome Robinson—of computerized rodeo entries, stock selection, and listing of point award results. By PRCA-membership card number. Not last name.

But Tom Ferguson did win the World in 1975. And he won it in the ninth steer wrestling go-round in Oklahoma City. By four-tenths of a second.

Those marbles, too, are his.

When Mel Hyland Rode Reckless Red

The kid from Canada stood on the hard-packed dirt behind the chute, looking at the big sorrel bronc standing nearly wither-high to the box. Mel Hyland was eighteen. It was his first year to follow the professional circuit. Here at Cheyenne, where winners in times past had been declared world champions, he had made it to the finals. In eighth place, but he had made it. His one big chance to add his name to that honor roll of bronc riding greats was the tall sorrel in the chute before him.

Mel's gaze took in the trim head, long neck, high wither, and extreme length of shoulder on the horse Harry Knight had named Reckless Red. His brand was 5B8. He was a Dakota bronc with throughbred lineage, one of Casey Tibbs's "Born to Buck" animals. Tibbs's partner Joe Schomer had called him Moreau River, after the range where the gelding had been foaled nine years before. The rangy bronc, stout for his twelve hundred pounds, pitched with hanging, aerial leaps, kicking over his head—an honest horse, one a man could win money on. If he hustled.

The kid eased onto the platform on the backside of the chute, sturdy halter in his left hand, the inch-thick woven hackrein draped over his shoulder. As the bronc dropped his head, Mel

Mel Hyland and Reckless Red, Houston 1975. *Photo by Jerry Gustafson, courtesy Mel Hyland*

slid his right arm over the neck, reaching under to grasp the halter. Then, slowly with both hands, he slipped the halter forward under the jaw, finally trapping the bobbing muzzle in the sheepskin-padded noseband. With deft fingers he latched the halter's headstrap over the poll, then laid the manila hemp rein over the red neck to tuck it out of the way, under the right side of the halter, before dropping to the worn path behind the chutes.

His old bronc saddle, an association-approved "committee rig," was lying on the ground, stirrup leathers forward, oxbow

stirrups tilted out. With leather worn to an ebony patina and scarred from battles lost, the basketweave-stamped Hamley rig was nearly as old as the kid who now took his seat against the cantleboard. Mel grasped the pommel, patched over where once there had been a saddle horn, and shoved the oxbows deep against his bootheels.

Tilting the rig first to one side and then the other, he swung each leg through the spurring lick, front to cantle, cantle to front, toes turned sharply outward, testing each stirrup length and bind against his leg.

And riding the big Dakota sorrel in his mind. Charging. Spurring with every leap.

Mel had learned to ride by relying on the spurring motion of his legs. The length of the stirrup leathers was critical. Buckled one hole too short, the stirrups could shove his legs up over the pommel's bulges or "swells," catapulting him out of the saddle. One hole too long, the stirrups could flop loose from his boots, leaving him helpless to react. Extra chunks of leather were shimmed against the buckle tongue, giving a "half-a-hole" adjustment for that just-right feel.

Mel turned the saddle on its side, lifting the short saddle skirts for another inspection of the narrow straps, or "binds," that checked the movement of the stirrup leather loop about its mooring. He couldn't be too careful. Too much was at stake.

The young bronc rider turned to his canvas war bag and fished out his ancient Crockett spurs. Ground down, rewelded where metal had cracked with fatigue, the spurs were ugly but they served their purpose. The short shanks, cocked inward, held free-spinning small dull star-rowels. He snugged the spurs to his boots with straps buckled over the outside of the arch and a whang leather thong under the front of the bootheel.

Mel unrolled his hand-me-down chaps—swapped by a bareback rider as too heavy—and buckled the belt at the front. Reaching behind, he carefully drew the three fasteners tightly about each thigh. A bronc rider couldn't afford to have his chaps squirm around his legs or bunch up against the saddle swells.

The kid settled once more into the saddle on the ground, gripping the swells between his legs. With an old sock for a sack he dabbed powdered rosin on the inside of each thigh. Then with the heels of his hands he shoved the saddle front downward through his leg grip. Again and again until the rosin squeaked with the heat of friction. And then he quit. Mel didn't want his spurring motion restricted by chaps half-glued to saddle swells.

54

He hadn't learned to ride that way, squeezing the saddle in default of swinging in rhythm with the motions of the bronc. And he wouldn't be here if he had.

Mel delayed as long as he could before placing his saddle on Reckless Red. The less time the bronc was encumbered in the chute, the better he would buck in the contest. And Reckless Red was keyed, like the runner at the line, his coat darkened with the sweat of anticipation, his lip quivering.

The saddle teetered on the break of the sorrel's withers as Mel reached a hooked wire through the backside slats to catch the front cinch ring dangling on the other side. He threaded the left latigo through the cinch ring and pulled up the slack. Twice he loosely looped the worn leather strap between the saddle ring and the cinch before hitching it back against the saddle ring, under the last pass. Tucking the loose latigo tail under the saddle, the kid turned to feather his building tension with calisthenics.

As the announcer turned the spectators' attention to the saddle bronc riding, Mel again extended the wire hook under the bronc's belly, this time hooking the buckle of the rear saddle cinch. Centered underneath, a length of whang leather "hobbled" the rear cinch strap to the front cinch to prevent it from slipping and pulling the saddle back during the ride. Mel latched the buckle in the bottom hole and climbed the chute to stand above Reckless Red. Careful not to touch the bronc's sensitive belly with his spurs, the rider eased down to firm footing on the gate and backside chute board. Mel grasped the pommel and pushed the saddle forward to the break of the withers, drawing a stirrup forward to see that his foot could reach around Red's long shoulder. He held the saddle in place while another cowboy tightened the left front cinch strap with a steady pull. Mel tested the tightness, tugging upward on the saddle front. Too loose, the saddle could roll and slip. Too tight, the horse could not buck freely. Again he tucked the latigo tail under the saddle, safely away from where a spur could hang up.

Mel glanced out into the arena. The bronc rider in the chute before him was nodding for the gate. Mel pulled the rear cinch just slightly snug and again hooked the buckle in the strap.

Moving to the front of the chute, he grasped the cheek strap of Reckless Red's halter and, pulling the hackrein back across the middle of the saddle, he hauled the bronc's head around straight. He clasped his left hand around the hemp rein, the heel of his fist butted up against the backside of the pommel, his thumb extended out along the rein. There on the rein, at the tip of his thumb or an inch beyond, would be where a rider should take his grip on an "average" bronc.

But Reckless Red was too long in the neck, with too much shoulder, to give an average rein. With the first drop of his head he could jerk a rider forward to the ground. Mel clenched the rein with his right hand, the forefinger knuckle butted up against the extended left thumb. At the end of this added measure, at the heel of his right fist, was where he would hold the rein on Reckless Red. Plucking a few strands from the bronc's red mane he tied a marker into the hemp plait.

The time had come for the announcer to call his name.

The gate men watched the kid's face. The chute boss stood by, the tail of Red's loose flank strap in his hand. The judges moved to either side of the gate, eyes fixed on the latch, clipboards and pencils in hand. The timers cradled the stopwatches in their hands.

Mel eased into the saddle as Reckless Red slammed his rump back against the chute, gathering his legs beneath him. Folding his chaps back, the rider slipped his feet into the stirrups and drew them back even with the cinch. With his left hand he clinched the hackrein in a "three-finger" grip, his little finger tucked beneath, even with the whisp of mane he'd used as a marker.

Mel held out the rein, drawing it across the sorrel's neck. Sighting over his extended wrist at the two red ears beyond, he drew his breath and nodded for the gate.

The bronc soared upward from his crouch. The rider's feet pumped forward, toes turned outward to the points of the compass, clapping his spurs against Reckless Red's neck, then sliding back, and then catching on the upward-driving shoulders. Mel's teeth gritted as his back was slammed against the chute support. For an instant the bronc hung in the air, a crescent silhouetted above the yawning gate, the kid perched like a solar flare on an eclipsed sorrel sun.

Slowly, Reckless Red sank back to earth, dropping to his haunches beside the two judges, to once more gather his legs beneath him. To the kid's surprise the bronc lunged forward to break into a run. Then came the sickening realization: His spurs were breaking loose from the points of the shoulders, slipping back with the drive of the horse. Past warnings of his mentors flashed through the young man's brain: "Never pull your feet out of the front end till he bucks." Clenching his fist, straining, lifting on the rein, he forced his feet back forward against the tugging force. Inch by agonizing inch.

Just when Mel's spur rowels rolled over the points of Red's long shoulders, the rangy bronc dropped his head between his legs and hit stiff-kneed, sucking back, heels cracking sharply behind. Instantaneously, Mel's thighs jammed into the saddle swells, the stirrups slapped against his bootheels. The storm had broken.

Now the bronc's hind legs recoiled, hammering the ground like pile drivers, lifting the horse and rider in a mighty leap. Mel's spurs again broke over the points of the shoulders. He squeezed his legs with all his might, ankles bent at right angles, to bear against his spurs. Dragging the dull rowels through the hair. Resisting the power thrust. His free arm swung forward in counterbalance. His left arm held the rein aloft, across the sorrel neck.

Higher and higher the tall bronc arched. Mel's feet popped free at the taper of the belly to swing upward to the cantle. His balance was forward, in line with the drive of the animal beneath him. His knees gripped the swells. His shoulder tensed, lifting on the rein.

At the peak of the leap Red humped in the middle, his head disappearing from the rider's view. Mel strained upward on the rein, swinging his free arm back, driving his feet forward to the shoulder in a slashing sweep. The bronc's heels snapped high above his head, jamming the kid's outturned feet against the oxbows, his legs against the swells, his buttocks hard against the saddle seat. The young rider's heart surged with exhilaration. He had beaten the bronc to the punch. He was in time. He was "tapped off." He hardly felt the jolt of Reckless Red's front feet slamming into the ground.

The bronc pitched upward, his ascent nearly vertical. Mel tilted forward, pushing the rein ahead, dragging his spurs across the shoulders, along the belly. His ankles were bent to the extreme, his toes nearly pointing to the back, so great was the friction against his spur rowels. Then, as Reckless Red once more capsized forward, plunging to the earth, the bronc rider tugged upward on the rein to force his feet forward, driving for the shoulders before the horse could hit the ground. The sorrel bronc's descent was nearly as vertical as his leap. The powerful kick of his heels accelerated the momentum of the rider's legs. His feet shot forward over the shoulders and up the bronc's neck. His right foot into the auburn mane. His left foot over the top of the hackrein.

Mel's feet slipped back with the impact of Red's landing. His left spur caught on the rein. The young rider's exhilaration froze in his throat. Again, the counsels of the past echoed in his mind: "Bear your rein across the neck. Don't give it any slack. Don't let it trap your foot."

Mel's shoulder flexed. White knuckles shoved the hackrein taut across the extended neck. His spurred boot flipped free and carried through its backward arc.

Cresting over, the sorrel slung his head against the rein and pitched over sideways in a sunfish roll. His right shoulder rose to meet a driving spur. His left shoulder dropped away. Mel's saddle lurched forward toward the hackrein with the motion. The kid fought for his balance against the catapulting force. Stretching out his arm. Then recoiling, lifting on the rein. Countertwisting with his body. Scrambling for a spurhold. Collecting the saddle swells between his thighs.

Then, twisting catlike in descent, the bronc rolled back beneath the scratching rider on his back.

Reckless Red lunged upward in spectacular arching leaps, leaving the ground four, five feet below his airborne hooves. Then banking clockwise to the right. Sweeping his mighty neck to work against the hackrein. Tucking forward, or turning over with sensational sunfish rolls. Kicking to the sky. Flashing his sorrel belly at the crowd, many now on their feet. Cheering. Screaming to the plucky little rider, the unknown Canadian kid.

Mel Hyland knew he couldn't weaken, couldn't hesitate for the slightest fraction of a second. It was not the fear but the heady thrill of flying that carried him ahead of the awesome thrust. His muscles ached from the exertion. Squeezing with every sinew from his hips to his feet. Dragging his spurs in their sweep from shoulder to cantle. Tilting his torso forward. Resisting the tremendous lunging power. Then heaving upward on the rein. Lifting. Arcing his free arm back. Balancing against the lurching sideroll. Hustling, slashing his feet forward, their momentum carrying his spurs high on the neck. Then slipping back to the crashing jolt of hooves against arena dirt. Pushing the rein across the neck. Bearing tension to free his spur from the rein-trap.

His motions were rhythmic. In perfect fluid time with the awesome pitching of the outlaw horse.

The blare of the buzzer was nearly lost to the roar of the cheering crowd. Mel looked down from his lofty seat to see the pickup men ride in on either side. His feet dropped to the cinch. With his free arm he grabbed for the front of his saddle. The power of the horse transmitted up his arm and snatched at his neck. The man on his left seized his hackrein to snub the bronc up short with a dally wrap around his saddle horn. Mel kicked free of the oxbows and released his grip on the saddle to dive to the safety of the pickup horse, his arms encircling the horseman's waist. As the rider on the right reached out, tripping loose the bronc's flank strap, Mel lit on his feet, the pickup horse between him and the plunging Reckless Red. The ride was over.

Mel stood transfixed, staring in deep respect at the sorrel bronc being led from the arena. Dwarfed by the thunderous, rolling applause, a numbness in his limbs, he turned to stumble over the cloddy ground to the cluster of jubilant cowboys at the chutes.

The record books read: 1967 Cheyenne Frontier Days Saddle Bronc Champion, Mel Hyland, Salmon Arm, British Columbia.

But more, much more than that. History was made in Cheyenne that day. Those present had witnessed one of the classic bronc rides of all time, when Mel Hyland rode Reckless Red.

Laying the Trip Fantastic

September winds swept down across the mile-high plains, alternately buffeting dust and rain across the plowed arena on the outskirts of Laramie. Standing pastern-deep in soft earth, the bay quarter horse held his head low, enduring the hardship, waiting his turn in the long box beside the narrow roping chute.

A lanky horseman hunkered over the bay, shielding his face from the gusts of blowing dirt. The man didn't look like the 1970 New Mexico Athlete of the Year, but then he didn't have to advertise. Here at the 1974 National Steer Roping Finals, Olin Young was the man to beat. All year he had been the man to beat.

The wiry six-footer from Peralta, New Mexico, was a seasoned twenty-year veteran of roping competition. His consistency was legend among his competition. Olin had taken the NFR calf roping four times, beginning with the very first National Finals in Dallas at the close of the 1959 season, when he was twenty-two. He also won the steer-roping finals in his very first year in that event, 1967, and the world championship, his first and long overdue crown, in 1971. This year had all the makings of a replay.

61

Olin's bay gelding Rocky was the proverbial gift horse, actually given to Young by roper Rick Sarah, who had been injured and was unable to continue competition. But where gift horses are concerned, the old bromide didn't apply to Rocky. Foaled Mister Bartrock, by Rocky Knock out of Katy Burt, the bay was a professional, carrying Olin to a record $9,415 pre-Finals total, at just ten rodeos. He was built for the role: heavy bones and muscling, deep chest through the heart, long shoulders, and withers shaped to hold a saddle against the pull of a rope. He was tall, 15 hands, and 1,300 pounds stout.

The steer Olin had drawn was prodded up the alley into the chute. He was a big animal, tipping the scales near 750 pounds. His wide horns were heavy at their base, solid for roping. His ample belly evidenced a prosperous summer. Kenny Call of Blanco, Texas, Olin's closest rival in the title race, had made a successful 17.4-second run on the steer the previous day, despite the wind. It had been good enough for a fourth place in the second go-round.

But to win in this, the seventh go, Olin Young would have to be quicker, much quicker. His perennial rival Sonny Davis, who was in hot contention for the average, already had wrapped one up in 13.6 seconds, the fastest time of the two-day competition. On the line were $458 and a good deal of pari-mutuel betting among the enthusiasts who had ignored the weather to crowd around the roping field.

With the twenty-three-foot length of 7/16-inch Dacron polyester rope securely moored to the horn of the Ryon saddle that he himself had designed, Olin built his loop, feeding rope through the honda lined with a knee-leather burner, until a four-foot circle was created. A quarter circle back from the honda he gripped the loop and a spoke of the slack line leading to the coils in his left hand. The pigging string—a seven-foot length of 7/16-inch

Olin Young and Rocky, Laramie NSRF 1974. *Photo by Dave Allen*

grass rope with a slip loop built into one end—lay convoluted under his belt, in easy reach.

From the barrier line the deep box measured twenty-five feet. In the arena dirt, fifteen feet beyond the bat-wing gates of the chute, lay the scoreline the steer must reach before triggering the barrier with the cord strung from his neck. Olin parked Rocky with his rump in the far corner, angling to face the steer's point of release. He was deliberate in his preparation. Consistent performance is not grounded in wasted motion and hasty decision. Quick always comes after Correct. Olin curled his fingertips over the slanted saddlehorn cap, waited until the steer concentrated on his escape, then called for cattle.

The race was on: the steer for the scoreline; Rocky to the barrier. It was a race Olin timed to lose, just by a hairbreadth.

Olin's right arm was in the air, the large loop swirling, tilting upward above his head—just the opposite of that of the team roper—rotating with the steady roll of his wrist. The circle grew with the slack fed through his fingers, through the honda. He was ready. Waiting to strike.

Rocky charged in pursuit. Body stretched out. Low to the ground. Hooves skimming the earth.

Then he was there. Behind the steer. Directly in line. Now rating off. Locking on his target. His nose nearly touching the prey.

Smoothly, deliberately, Olin's arm swept forward. Releasing the loop from the palm of his hand. Then following through. Pointing to the target. The bobbing, corriente horns.

The loop settled. Catching under the base of the right horn. The slack in the loop traveling. Curling. Enclosing the left horn. Then completing its global trip. Returning home. To the base of the right horn. To the waiting honda.

Still Rocky held his trailing position. Waiting for his rider's cue.

Olin drew the slack down the steer's right side, dipping the rope under the round belly. He reined Rocky aside. Forty-five degrees to the left. Then urged the bay forward.

Passing by, he fished his line behind the steer's right hock. The trip was set.

Rocky accelerated in rapid response, his ears laid back, his neck stretched out. He hit the end of the line. Never flinching. Never breaking step. Never veering from his course. His massive muscles pulsed with the effort. His chest, shoulders, hips, gaskins bulged with the power of his drive.

The steer was stopped with the jolt. His head whipped to the right. Following the honda. Down his side. Around the fulcrum of his hocks.

He was airborne. His legs tripping straight out. The snatch of the rope traveling, whiplashing down his spine. His body whirling. Flipping. Rolling in the air. Landing in the soft ground. On his right side. Over his back. On his left side. Stunned.

Olin swung his right leg back over the low cantle, clear of the rope. Rocky leaned deeper into the breast harness. Showing his heart. His try. Holding course. Low to the ground. Tugging. Driving with his hind quarters. Dragging, logging the weight through the deep soil.

The steer was towing straight behind the laboring horse. Olin was dismounting on the left. Running down the taut rope. Unraveling the pigging string from his belt. Jumping over the rope. To the right. To the steer's legs. Into position for the tie. Hollering "Whoa!"

Rocky ground to a stop, leaned forward against the burden at the end of the rope.

The pigging string was in Olin's left hand. His right hand was grabbing the steer's lower left leg. The noose was encircling the animal's hoof, slipping up his leg, halfway to the knee.

Olin tugged the noose tight. Drew the string back. To the rear of the steer. Under the hind legs. Swung it over the legs. Pulling, walking them forward. Sliding in the cradle of the grass string.

His left knee was bearing down on the steer's flank. Holding it steady. Resisting a kick. He held the string upward with his left hand. Taut. His right hand slid down the line, the heel of his hand holding against the gathered legs.

Bearing slight weight on the animal's hip and leg with his left leg, Olin stepped forward with his right. The steer's legs resting on his left foot. Balancing. Squaring with the prostrate steer.

With both hands he wrapped the taut string full around the two hind legs and the front leg drawn back with the noose. Gathering them. Binding them together.

A second wrap. Around the hind legs. Short-cutting the rearward projecting front leg. Into a half hitch, pulled tight by the waiting fingers of his left hand.

The steer was tied. In 13.4 seconds.

First the go-round, then the World. Laramie, and the Steer Roping World Championship for 1974, belonged to Olin Young.

Dar la Vuelta

Dar la vuelta, to take a turn. A horseman pursues the fleeing steer, roping the beast by the horns. His partner follows in tandem, snaring the animal's heels. Each wraps the loose end of his rope about the saddlehorn—*dar la vuelta*. They face each other in triumph, the wild steer suspended at bay between the taut ropes.

There is no more magnificent display of precision performance by men and horses than the artful execution of "dally" team roping.

Sport of the Californios from the halcyon days of the Mission ranchos, dally team roping has been the most rapidly growing horseback sport in America. Within the ranks of rodeo professionals, dally roping quickly spread from California to rodeos across the nation, coming into its own with the 1973 National Finals Rodeo, to never again share the limelight with its "hard-and-fast" team-tying counterpart of Texas origin.

And in the televised final go-round in that premiere year for nationwide NFR television coverage, the masterful exhibition of the dally left an indelible imprint on the minds of an American public "turned on" to a new dimension of televised sports spectaculars.

By the end of the nine go-rounds immediately preceding that memorable Sunday afternoon in December, not a single go-round in the tandem roping had been won by a time in excess of 7.3 seconds. Less than eight-tenths of a second separated the top three teams. Leroy and Doyle Gellerman, the father-and-son combination from San Jose, led the pack with 93.8 seconds on nine head of the Mexican corriente, or "common" steers, one-tenth of a second ahead of Dan Branco of Chowchilla and his header John Wilken of New Mexico. Californians Jim Rodriguez, Jr., and Ken Luman stood third in the contest with a total time of 94.6. The stage was set for a roping duel; it would be the story of the quick and the dead.

The draw for timed event stock in the final go-round of the 1973 National Finals at Oklahoma City was conducted one hour before the rodeo began. In the team roping, Jim Rodriguez and Ken Luman drew the worst of the lot. A brindle animal with wide, flat horns, their Mexican corriente had a pattern of ducking to the right, away from the header's loop, once he had gained the freedom of the arena. In the eighth go-round, his last previous appearance, the devious beast had caused the thirty-year veteran and former world champion Les Hirdes and his partner John Deaton to draw a no-time. Not one team had placed on the steer throughout the rodeo.

Jim Rodriguez and Ken Luman had drawn better, but they also had seen worse in their ten-year association as a roping team. Rodriguez was an athlete of immense natural ability and skill with the header's loop. At eighteen, with offers of a base-ball career coming in from the Washington Senators and the reigning World Series champion New York Yankees, Jim elected to devote his talents to the rodeo arena. With the great Gene

Jim Rodriguez, Jr. and Ken Luman, NFR 1973. *Courtesy* Western Horseman

Rambo—his future father-in-law—picking up the heels, Rodriguez roped his way to the 1959 World Team Roping Championship. He became the youngest world champion in the history of professional rodeo. Now, fourteen years later, Jim Rodriguez had made it to every national team roping finals since.

Jim's partner, the six-foot Luman, was an artist with the heel loop. In 1963, when Gene Rambo retired from the grueling life of the full-time professional rodeo, Rodriguez had asked Luman to join him. The combination clicked, they were formidable competition. Three additional times Rodriguez had claimed the world title; Ken Luman, once.

Before the performance, Luman and Rodriguez laid out their strategy. If their competition posted slow times, they would play it safe. Luman, the heeler, in breaking from the box to the steer's right, would haze the uncooperative animal into position to give Rodriguez the perfect shot at the horns, before dropping back for his heel loop. If their closest competitors were fast, they would have to gamble on the fast break, the rapid throw.

Choice vanished when Dan Branco and Lefty Wilken stretched out their steer in eight seconds flat. Two runs later the Geller-mans took the flag in 7.4 seconds, giving the father-son team a commanding lead in the average with an unbelievable 101.2 seconds total. To overtake them, Jim Rodriguez and Ken Luman would have to post a 6.5-second run on the brindle steer that ducked to the right.

And neither man was mounted on his own horse.

Jim Rodriguez was using Les Hirdes's bay gelding, Cowboy. At 15 hands and 1,200 pounds, the bay quarter horse possessed the characteristics that made a good heading horse. With a fairly small head and average length neck, he gave his rider a clear view of his target. Well-developed withers held a saddle solid against the jolt and stress of stopping and turning cattle. Cowboy was agile but strong, solid boned and heavily muscled in the V of his chest, and in the hips, thighs, and gaskins—where it counts. And he worked cattle with finesse.

Ken Luman was mounted on Frank Ferriera's sorrel, Whiskey. In contrast to Cowboy, the sorrel quarter horse gelding was lighter, "more agile, smoother moving," with less muscle in the shoulders and chest. His comparable height, 15 hands, gave Luman the perfect angle at a steer's heels, and heavy muscling in the hips and hind legs "gave him the power to hold against the pull of a steer and head horse." Whiskey was quiet and well mannered, responding instantly to a light rein, with the understanding of a true stock horse.

Both horses were outfitted with roping saddles, with the back cinch hobbled forward to avoid the sensitive flanks and to better distribute the roping strain. The four-inch throat of each saddlehorn was wrapped with a band from an inner tube, to give the dally wraps a "bite" against the pull of a steer. The saddle pads were thick for protection of withers and back; Luman's was of the popular Cool Back type, invented by a team-roping Montana physician. The pad was filled with polyurethan and covered with Kodel, a spun glass material developed to keep hospital patients dry and free of bedsores. To keep the horses' attention on the job at hand, each one was equipped with a breast collar and tie-down to the halter. The more high-strung Cowboy was outfitted with a medium port bit equipped with a roller to work with his tongue. Whiskey had a spade bit.

Rodriguez and Luman also differed in their selection of ropes, the tools of the roper's trade. For the severe stresses of heading, Rodriguez preferred a 30-foot, 7/16 diameter nylon rope with a hard twist or "lay" in its construction. For his 35-foot heeling loop Luman used the smaller 3/8-inch nylon with the softer medium lay. At the business end of each prestretched and waxed nylon line, the honda—through which the tail passes in forming the loop—was lined with a protective "burner" of hard leather, rather than with the rawhide used by many calf ropers.

Mounting the borrowed horses, each roper placed the bridle reins deep within the palm of his left hand, the excess rein passing over the top of the fist, with the fingers free to cradle the forward coils of the rope. The tool's tail was laid out of the way on the left side of the saddle.

With his right hand, each man shook out his loop, the size determined by its purpose: Rodriguez's heading loop made a four-foot diameter circle; Luman's heeling loop was half again as large. The loop was grasped along with a length or "spoke" of tail so that the honda lay a quarter circle forward on the loop. In the grip, only the forefinger remained free, to guide the roping action.

Their preparation took only seconds, but to Leroy and Doyle Gellerman the suspense was agony. Money, $1184.54 to be exact, for the go-round and average payoffs, lay tantalizingly, a single run from their reach.

Six-and-a-half seconds. Could Rodriguez and Luman do it? On the steer with the perfect record in crushing NFR hopes?

In living rooms across the nation, people who had never before seen a rodeo dropped what they were doing, turned their attention to the television screen, completely fascinated with the drama unfolding in Oklahoma City.

The ropers rode into the roping boxes—Luman to the right; Rodriguez, the header, to the left—and circled to face the troublesome brindle steer.

The steer fidgeted within the confines of the narrow chute. Cowboy backed against the welded pipes sixteen short feet behind the barrier stretched taut before him, his head straight ahead, responsive to the light touch of the restraining rein, craving the chase.

In the opposite box Whiskey stood quietly, Ken Luman's light hand the only barrier between him and the arena beyond. Luman watched his partner's face with a steady gaze, waiting for his signal.

The gate man's eyes, too, were fixed on Rodriguez, watching for the nod that would send the lever in his right hand forward, the gates open, the corriente steer free.

Jim saw the steer was ready. With the loop held deep in his hand he cupped his fingertips around the saddlehorn, tensed in his stirrups, shifted his gaze to measure the steer's escape with the yardstick of the barrier pin.

And nodded his head.

For better or worse, the brindle steer was theirs.

The steer moved out. Horns rattled against metal. Cloven hooves churned through soft arena dirt. The roping horses stood their ground, craving to chase the hollow rattle of retreating dew claws.

The steer's hip passed the barrier pin. Jim turned the bay horse loose.

Ten, twelve, thirteen feet. The steer lunged past the score line, tripping the barrier in Cowboy's face, leaving the neck cord broken in the dirt.

Ken Luman urged Whiskey into action, pouring on the power, closing in on the steer and the bay.

True to form, the corriente angled for the right arena wall. Rodriguez laid the rein across Cowboy's neck, urging him to the right. Short-cutting the path of the fleeing beast. Jim's right arm was up, his elbow high, the loop describing a flat circle, counterclockwise above his head.

Cowboy thundered down on the steer, then rated off. His nose was even with the animal's left hip, a scant yard away. The position was perfect. Rodriguez launched the rope forward with a sidearm throw. Smoothly delivering the loop from the base of his palm. His forefinger pointing the way, in the deliberate follow-through. Like a major league pitcher.

The loop flew perfectly flat to its target. Encircling the widespread horns. Then snubbing against the base of the right horn. The slack of the loop traveled flat and egg-shaped, around to the waiting honda behind the left horn. Absent was the figure-eight curl so characteristic of softer ropes, harder throws. Here was the soft touch of the artist, the master.

Jim watched the loop find its target; then, with palm turned downward, he grasped the rope and jerked it straight back past his right knee. The slack came out of the loop, the line whirring through the honda burner. The rope tightened in a perfect two-horn catch.

In a reflex born of practice, Rodriguez rolled his wrist, turning his thumb upward out of the way. He drew the rope across the front of the saddle. With a blur of motion he wrapped his dallies around the saddlehorn. His thumb up. His eyes never leaving the brindle steer.

Cowboy set his feet into the ground with the catch and leaned away from the action. The steer instantaneously hit the end of the rope. Dallies bit into rubber hornwrap. With one fluid power drive of coordinated motion the bay horse took the shock against his withers and quartered in a left lead across the arena, stopping the steer in its tracks, bending its neck around, leading the plunging animal away to the left.

Jim turned to watch his heeler work.

After clearing the box, Whiskey raced to intercept the roping action. Ken Luman's right arm was held high. His wide loop tilted downward in a circle over his left shoulder. The sorrel moved in straight behind the lunging steer, his blazed face even with the steer's left hip. With the set of the head horse, Whiskey had his rider directly behind the steer's heels. Five feet away. In perfect position for the heel loop.

Luman's second swing was synchronized with the leap of the steer as Rodriguez led the animal away to the left. The heels rose out of the dirt. Ken's arm came forward and down, with constant speed. The loop stood on edge, ahead of the animal's hind legs.

Bending from the momentum, the loop curved under the steer's belly. The position of the honda behind the right hip and hock held the loop open—a trap for the descending heels.

Whiskey stopped level. Muscles bunched, anticipating the

74

action. Luman stood, his weight over his right stirrup. Watching. Waiting for the hooves to drop through the open loop. They were there. He clenched the rope. Jerked it high above his face, his thumb held upward.

The loop drew tight, snaring the two hind legs.

The steer's forward momentum drew the line straight. Luman dropped his hand, thumb up, across the front of the saddlehorn. Never taking his eyes off his heel loop, he whipped his dally wraps—dar la vuelta—counterclockwise around the saddlehorn.

Jim Rodriguez saw Ken dally. Quickly he spun Cowboy in a reverse to the right. The horses faced. The ropes pulled taut, straight in line, the steer suspended between. The run on the brindle steer was finished.

The ropers craned their necks. Checked the barrier judge. They were OK. The clock. Above their heads. The electronic arena clock. Flashing. Showing their time, their official time: 5.8 seconds. An unbelievable, National Finals Rodeo record 5.8 seconds.

Two hats floated into the air. Flotsam in the thunderous tide of jubilee.

Jimmie and Billy

"Valley Veterinary Service." The veterinary technician cradled the telephone on her shoulder, drying her hands.

"Hello. This is Jimmie Gibbs. Is Dr. Van Zandt there?" It was long distance. The voice on the other end of the line was pressed.

Doug Van Zandt, D.V.M., picked up the phone.

"Doctor?" The veterinarian immediately recognized the familiar resonance of the rodeo drawl.

"It's Billy. He's having problems breathing and he's off his feed."

"Where are you, Jimmie?"

"We're in Nampa, Idaho. Mom's with me. We came down from Sheridan, and by the time we got here, he was off his feed. I drew us out of the barrel race and took him to the vet here. He said it was a respiratory infection and treated him with tetracycline. But he's just not responding, Dr. Van Zandt."

"Is he running a fever?"

"Yes, and it's getting worse."

Doug Van Zandt rubbed a strong hand over cropped grey hair. He squinted through his bifocals, picturing the situation for the petite brown-haired young woman and her quarter horse, a thousand rodeo miles from her home in Valley Mills, Texas. Noting everything that was said, he mentally checked off the list of symptoms.

"Can you bring him here? I think we'd better have a look at him, Jimmie." The soft voice and sincere, professional tone of the practitioner veiled a mounting concern.

"How soon can you get here?"

Jimmie and Blevins Gibbs threw their clothes into the Ford pickup, loaded Billy into his stylish goose-neck trailer, filled up with gas at the self-service pump, and wheeled onto Interstate-80. Six hundred miles to backtrack. Speed limit, 55 MPH. Watching the speed. Scanning ahead, checking the rear view, then back to the red speedometer needle. Pushing Praying. Pulling Billy to help in Hardin, Montana.

Hot wind. Cold coffee. Nervous talk and country music sucked out the window to roll with tires trilling, ticking like a study-hall clock. Road signs rising, sliding away; green flashes flickering in gray waves of heat. Hallucinations in a hideous slow motion dream.

Mountains peeking over the horizon. Rising. Looming. Canyons opening, closing to passes, dropping, winding past the ranks of pine trees standing at attention.

West Yellowstone. Stopping. Unloading Billy, visibly weakening. A man yelling, shouting, threatening on the street. Reloading the sick horse. Tugging. Shoving. Billy staggering, stumbling into the trailer.

Out onto the road again. Up 191. Over the hump. Wending the Gallatin. Through Bozeman Pass. Down from the Rockies and down the Yellowstone of John Colter's hellish race for life.

Southeastern Montana and Hardin, awash in amber waves of July grain. The heat was oppressive. As Doug Van Zandt went about his work, he found his mind turning to dwell on

Jimmie and Billy, NFR 1976. *Photo by Bern Gregory, courtesy* World of Rodeo

the girl and her horse Billy. How long had it been since he had first noticed Jimmie and Billy on the rodeo circuit? Seven years? Eight?

Doug Van Zandt had gone to vet school later in life than many of his colleagues. First there had been a tour of the rodeo road, dreams of a championship that never would be. Then he had volunteered for duty to his country, serving in the navy through the Korean "police action." Athletic and barrel-chested, he had made the grade to become a SEAL, a frogman assigned to a stint with the Underwater Demolition Team. Later, he put in a tour as commander of a submarine.

After the service, he enrolled under the GI Bill in the college of veterinary medicine at Auburn University. While in college he had interned at Clarendon, Texas, before graduating in 1965.

By this time his bent toward equine medicine was set. Much of his practice was taken up with racetrack and rodeo work, and now, twenty years later, he was among the most highly respected practitioners in his field. Among those animals for whom he had become physician in residence were Warren Wuthier's calf-roping horse, Go Fast, and Walt Linderman's dogging team, Doug and Scott.

Of them all, he mused, only Walt Linderman's Scott had the amount of character that Jimmie Gibbs' Billy showed. Billy was an animal with personality and a whale of a lot of class. He was unbelievable, the veterinarian realized. He was probably the classiest, cool professional animal that he had ever had the pleasure of working with. He was just as calm and easy, and yet put him coming out of the alley to run cans, he was phenomenal. But as soon as that was over, he was right back to being the cool dude. That was Billy.

And Jimmie. Perhaps it was her personality that had rubbed off on the bay gelding. Or was it the other way around? Dr. Van Zandt believed it was a little bit of both.

Jimmie Gibbs was a world champion, a person of ultimate class, the practitioner continued in his reverie. Of course, when you knew her parents, then you could understand the situation. She didn't have any other way to go. Her father and mother were people with supreme class and integrity. Marvelous people. Her mother was a delight, the daughter of Colonel Zack Miller of the famous 101 Ranch and Wild West Show, and filled with more stories than you can imagine. And Jim Gibbs is the antithesis to that. Terrific dry sense of humor. Very quiet, very controlled. A man of impeccable integrity.

In 1975 Jimmie Gibbs had won four national titles. In the National Intercollegiate Rodeo Association, she was the barrel-racing champion and reserve all-around cowgirl, one step down from her NIRA diadem of the previous year. In the Girls Rodeo Association, she not only was the 1975 All-Around Champion, but also the champion calf roper and, by a commanding lead, the World Champion Barrel Racer.

In 1976 and 1977 she also led the GRA barrel racers in total points for the season, and in 1978 she had been runner-up. She had been to the top of the world, at an age when most young girls can only dream of being champions. And it was Billy who had carried her to the top.

Van Zandt first had come to know Jimmie Gibbs through his veterinary technician, Butch Bonine. Butch was the wife of champion saddle bronc rider J. C. Bonine. She was raised in a rodeo family, her brother Bud Munroe was the current leader of the saddle bronc riders, coming into the fall season in 1980. Butch Bonine herself was an accomplished horsewoman, riding her barrel horse Buckshot in GRA competition. Butch and Jimmie both had been directors of the GRA; Jimmie was just beginning her second two-year term as president of the rapidly growing association.

Butch had worked for Dr. Van Zandt for four years. When J. C. Bonine injured his knee in competition, he also began working for the veterinarian. The Bonines lived at the practitioner's home, part of the family. Jimmie Gibbs was drawn into the close-knit group as she became acquainted with Bud Munroe. Now, in 1980, Jimmie and Bud were engaged to be married.

And as he was doing Bonine's equine work, Dr. Van Zandt started seeing Jimmie and Billy occasionally. She would come by with Billy, as problems would come up. Over the years, Dr.

Van Zandt became physician in residence for the champion barrel horse, when the pair were traveling the Northwest. Billy was
number one in the Van Zandt equine family. No matter where
they were on the rodeo trail, they kept in touch. Even though
other practicioners along the line were to work on the bay gelding, Jimmie and Dr. Van Zandt always conversed back and forth.
If he caught the sniffles in Seattle, she'd call and they'd converse.

But this time it was no simple case of the sniffles. With a respiratory infection this far advanced, too many things could go
wrong. There were too many variables, too much at stake. Doug
Van Zandt was concerned, deeply concerned.

At last Jimmie Gibbs wheeled the pickup and horse trailer off
the blacktop and onto the gravel drive in front of the low, white
veterinary clinic.

As Jimmie backed Billy out of the immaculate trailer, Blevins
recapped for the vet the events leading up to their call. Jimmie
had been traveling with Lynn Manning, but Lynn was headed
for California. Blevins had flown up to be with Jimmie while
she worked the northern rodeos before heading back home. Jimmie and Billy had placed second, behind Lynn McKenzie, in
Laramie on the twelfth. That night in Billings at Bud Munroe's
place, Billy had left some of his oats uneaten. It was unchar-
acteristic of him not to clean up on his feed. By the time they
got to Nampa for that rodeo, July 15 to 19, the horse had not
picked up on his appetite.

It was at this time that Jimmie had a local veterinarian treat
the animal. He had used a low dosage of oxytetracycline. Billy
had not responded.

Now it was Sunday, July 20, in Hardin, Montana. As Jimmie
led Billy around, the horse was hardly able to walk. Even as ill
as he was, the vet noticed, Billy was a striking animal. He stood
15 hands and weighed 1,100 pounds, a well-proportioned quarter horse with trim, athletic lines. He had a pretty head, with

expressive eyes that spoke for his intelligence. His ears were attentive, following Jimmie's every move and word.

Immediately Dr. Van Zandt commenced his preliminary examination. Billy was spiking a high fever. The upper respiratory infection had advanced. There were indications of secondary complications from the oxytetracycline, a drug standard for the treatment of cattle but highly controversial in equine practice. Tissue necrosis in the throat may have occurred. He had a severe respiratory ailment that developed into a pleuritis, or profuse infection of the thoracic cavity.

Dr. Van Zandt did not immediately tell Jimmie and Blevins Gibbs the full gravity of Billy's situation. A condition such as evidenced here bore nearly a 100 percent fatality rate in the average horse population.

He did not, because Billy was not your average horse. Doug Van Zandt figured the odds were in Billy's favor, just by his personality.

The veterinarian cleared the decks and turned his full attention to Billy's battle for life. Realizing his own human shortcomings, the practitioner consulted with his colleague Dr. Lance Moxie in Sheridan, Wyoming, and had telephone hotlines put in both to Dr. Simon Turner and his staff at the Colorado State University School of Veterinary Medicine and Dr. Tom Vaughn at Auburn University. Doug Van Zandt knew he needed every bit of expertise he could drawn upon.

Billy's throat and thoracic area were badly embarrassed with the inflammation and swelling, so badly that all the medication and fluids given him had to go intravenously. The veterinarian found that he was unable to use the jugular veins that are normally used. With his technician, Van Zandt would have to sit underneath the horse and give him IV's in the large veins of his front or hind legs. Normally, an animal would get anxious and walk or pace, and after you IV them for a time, they don't appreciate it and they object or fight. Billy never moved.

All the while, Jimmie Gibbs, stayed by her horse, encouraging him in constant conversation. Her poise and courage, the practitioner thought, were remarkable, unknown in a girl her age. Although Doug Van Zandt had several top horsemen work for him over the years, he always had hired girls as veterinary technicians; he believed they were more intuitive about animals, either large or small. Animals seem to trust them a lot more, he mused. But Jimmie and Billy superseded that claim. It was just a relationship between two individuals.

It was uncanny. When Jimmie was with the horse, Billy was a totally relaxed individual. Always alert, but relaxed. Very easy going. The easiest horse to get along with that the practitioner had ever seen. But when Jimmie was with him, it was almost intuitive. He not only was relaxed, but he depended a lot on her, too. When she was there, Billy became just like any charged up, well-tuned horse, watching everything that goes on. They notice everything. You slam a door and they kind of snort back. And he was like that. But when she was there it was like tranquilization had set in. Total trust.

Two days after Dr. Van Zandt had begun treatment, Billy's fever broke. It was a major break. Spirits dared ever so slightly to rise. The veterinarian stayed with his patient, monitoring his vital signs, keeping the life-giving medications and fluids flowing. Blevins kept conversation going. Bud Munroe was there. Coffee literally ran through the old Bunn coffee maker in the clinic's Spartan waiting room with its square, black space heater, four fiberglass chairs and, on the wall to the side of the stove, a "Gaines Guide to America's Dogs" chart. Pictures of every breed of dog imaginable. Ninety-seven of them.

Jimmie constantly tended to the comfort of her horse. First and foremost, she knew that if she didn't have Billy . . .

And he realized it.

She'd be doing things, the veterinarian recalled, like cleaning his feet. She'd be talking to you, just be talking, and go over and pick up a hoof pick and just walk over to the side of him, and the foot would come up. There wasn't any bend-down-and-pull-it-up routine. And it was a totally relaxed thing; intuitive.

But Jimmie always had been attentive to her horse's needs, the vet mused. Before she would load him into that goose-neck trailer, she would carefully wrap his legs for protection. Traveling down the road, she'd make frequent stops, every two hundred miles or so, to let him out to stretch his legs and exercise. And it didn't matter if they were running late, Billy came first. Whenever they reached their destination, Billy's stall was found and his needs tended to before her own, no matter how tired or hungry she was.

Religiously, Jimmie fed her barrel horse on schedule, 7:30 a.m. and 4:30 p.m., never varying over a half hour if she could help it. Straight oats in the morning, and in the evening oats, sweet feed and bran, vitamins, salt mineral—electrolyte in hot weather—a liquid supplement for a blood builder, and a cup of soybean meal for his coat. Basically, a balanced diet and hay, grass hay.

She always provided time for Billy to digest what he ate before either competition or exercise, two to three hours, and maintained an exercise program. After thirteen years, barrel practice seldom was needed, but training kept him in top physical condition. Jimmie firmly believed that a barrel horse, like any athlete in competition, had to feel good and be in top shape in order to win.

And win he did. In 1976, Billy was picked as "Mr. Frontier Airlines." In 1978 he became the "Black Velvet Horse of the Year," the highest honor bestowed on a barrel horse. In 1979, the top finalists in the event voted the bay gelding "The Horse With The Most Heart," and in 1980, for the second time in his career, he was on his way toward claiming the event's highest recognition, a silver tray awarded in memory of the late Poco Excuse, Jeanna Day's 1974 champion barrel horse.

Over the past month alone, Jimmie had told the veterinarian, the pair had won over $7,000. Through the Fourth of July run they had won Greeley and Lander, and Dickinson and Killdeer, North Dakota—both in the same day—and had placed at Cody, Livingston, and at Crawford, Nebraska, before their second place run at Laramie the following week. It had been the best Fourth she'd ever had with Billy.

Billy, the vet remarked, was an athlete of supreme quality. The longer she hauled that bugger, the better he got. It was phenomenal. Normally it's the reverse: the more miles you put on them, they just keep falling off. As any good athlete does. They reach their peak and start going down. And the rodeo season is a long one. The great horses—and all your great horses have it— they've got that little extra try, and they give it every time they run. Even when they don't always feel like it, when they're a little sore, or when they've been hauled, or have run three times in three days before. When it comes time to run they forget about it and they give it that little extra try. Billy was like that.

That's not only in horses, he had observed, it's in people, too.

To see Jimmie and Billy run was really something. It was not like a horse and rider, but *horserider*. Their personalities were just perfectly matched.

You could see it before a run. Jimmie would begin to get ready, and Billy would get ready, too. He could feel the tension, sense it. And he would get pumped up. Anticipating, and just a little nervous. But always levelheaded, the cool dude.

In starting a run down the alley, Billy automatically would shift into his right lead, anticipating the right turn around the first barrel in the cloverleaf pattern. A consummate horsewoman, Jimmie would be with him as one unit, through the approach, then slowing to collect his legs beneath him, and perfectly in line with the axis of his dipping centerline as they bent around the upright barrel.

As Billy would make that first turn and drive forward for the second barrel, Jimmie would automatically shift her weight forward, going with the animal's drive.

Shifting leads with Billy was so smooth, it was unnoticeable to the accomplished rider. It was action–reaction all the way, in a subtle combination of cue and move.

In his left lead, collecting himself into the second barrel, the bay gelding was at his best. It was almost unbelievable how he literally could snap around the second barrel. Billy's second barrel was legend among the horsewomen of the GRA. There wasn't any wasted motion or extra steps. It was all natural ability; there was no training an animal to make that move. It just came naturally. All Jimmie could contribute was to *be* there. Sliding her inside hand down the short rein loop along the inside of his neck, holding the calf of her inside leg tight against his body, shifting forward over his withers and staying straight with him as he churned out of the turn.

Then, keeping his left lead, Billy would reach out for the third barrel. Collect himself. Snap to. Then lunge, to stretch for the finish line, Jimmie with him, in reflex reaction.

It was Billy's tremendous heart that the veterinarian was counting on the pull the animal through the crisis of his life in the unrelenting July heat. Day and night, Doug Van Zandt stayed with Jimmie Gibbs and her horse Billy. Van Zandt, and Tom Vaughn and Simon Turner, human beings pooling all their resources to save this one magnificent animal.

Any other horse, the practitioner knew, any normal horse would have died within twenty-four hours of his arrival, given the condition Billy was in when he first examined him. But now, it was three days, going on four, and Billy still was holding on, his undying spirit still fighting.

On Thursday morning, Bud Munroe had to leave. He was up in the bronc riding at Cheyenne that afternoon. Jimmie and Blevins faced their vigil alone, with the unrelenting physician.

"If he just doesn't colic," Jimmie thought.

Dr. Van Zandt kept the great horse sedated to relieve the intense pain. As long as Jimmie and the soft-spoken doctor were present, Billy bore it all with patience, and trust.

Jimmie, too, put her faith in the gentle horse doctor, knowing he was doing all that could be done. Little was said; more was communicated in silence than anything else. Over the years, the grey-haired practitioner had come to an unspoken understanding with the girl and her horse. Jimmie didn't want Billy to suffer any more than was feasible to bring him back; she trusted that Doug Van Zandt would know.

By mid-morning, it was apparent that Billy's condition was deteriorating slowly. His vital systems were not fully functioning. The practitioner was seeing symptoms of possible liver damage, not unexpected from the animal's prolonged high fever.

Just before noon, as they were walking him, Billy got down. A secondary colic—paroxysmal pain in the abdomen and bowels—had hit. The great horse had reached the point of no return. Jimmie knew.

Dr. Van Zandt filled the syringe. With eyes clouded over, he put Billy to sleep.

"It was the hardest piece of work that I've ever had in my practice, was putting Billy down.

"They had done so much together . . . We'd kept track of them for so long . . . It was like losing a member of the family.

"But there wasn't really too much to be said."

Although the veterinarian offered to provide a burial spot for Billy there on the bench above the confluence of the Big Horn and the historic Little Big Horn, Jimmie elected to take Billy home to Texas.

"I don't think in the annals of horsedom that there has been a situation quite like it. It was during a real hot prolonged heat spell that we were having. It was spiking 106 and 110 down in Texas, and well over 100 here. So we loaded him in my pickup; we loaded the pickup full of Billy and dry ice. And wrapped him up. And headed out within thirty minutes to an hour after he expired.

"Two days later, I was in Valley Mills, Texas."

It was a small and subdued procession that made its way up the lane to the Gibbs ranch—the veterinarian and his technician in the truck that carried Billy; Jimmie and Blevins towing the empty horse trailer. There, on a hill out from the house they could see a mound of red and gray Texas soil beneath a spreading oak tree. Their arrival had been anticipated.

Jim Gibbs and the ranch hands, with Bud Munroe's help, had prepared for Billy's final resting place. Bud had called Hardin from Cheyenne, but had just missed them. They already had left for Texas. It had been hard for him at Cheyenne. He hadn't done well, couldn't get his mind on it. It was hard for anyone to get their mind on anything. He took the next plane out and had arrived at the ranch ahead of Jimmie. Now, Billy was to be laid to rest next to Bill, the old Ed Echols gelding that had prepared Jimmie for the time that she and Billy would ride to the top of the world.

Dr. Van Zandt pulled up and rigged his truck around. Pretty soon people started stopping by. Friends had come to pay their last respects. A crane lifted Billy from the truck and lowered him to rest on white beach sand lining the bottom of the grave. It was a tough time for those gathered there on the hill. A memorial service was held, then Jim Gibbs turned and quietly asked Doug Van Zandt to say the final blessing.

"After the funeral," the veterinarian recalled, "everyone just went into the house. We had a big meal, then went into their living room. Not much was said at first, one way or the other. We just sat around the living room. And it was a supremely comfortable thing. Their living room is Billy. You walk in and there are saddles, and trophies and buckles, on the tables, and pictures on the walls. Over the fireplace was a large portrait of Billy. You can't believe the profuse amount of things that this horse had accomplished.

"Bud was there. I think probably just by his presence he helped Jimmie, more than all the words that could be said, just by being there. At that time they were engaged to be married, and they were in love . . . The timing was just great.

"It was kind of a relaxed, easy thing," the practitioner said in looking back, "sitting around, hearing all the things that Billy had done. That's the way everybody unwound."

Blevins Gibbs recalled the first time she had laid eyes on Billy. She and Jimmie had gone down to Rebecca Tyler's place to try out another gelding, a Flit Bar horse that had shown promise. The bloodline included some accomplished animals in reining and cutting and in rodeo, and two of Jimmie's friends had acquired horses of the Flit Bar line.

While Jimmie tried out this horse, Blevins wandered about the Tyler's paddock. There, she discovered the bay gelding. Robin's Flit Bar was his registered name, and recalling it, Blevins at first couldn't really put her finger on it, but it was the alert, intelligent personality of the colt, not his physical stature or his way of going, that had caught her eye. But that was it, she insisted *that* was the colt they were looking for.

They went on home, then Jimmie phoned Rebecca back. Yes, the bay was a Flit Bar colt, too. They bought both animals.

Once at home in the Gibbs pasture, Robin's Flit Bar became Billy, in tribute to the Ed Echols horse that had carried Jimmie to over one hundred awards in horse shows and junior rodeo contests. Jimmie had the halter-broke colt fully broken and trained by family friend Marty Petska. After that, she mostly pasture rode him and worked him some in the cloverleaf barrel pattern until he was four.

When she graduated from high school in 1970, Jimmie was offered a rodeo scholarship by Sonny Sikes at Sam Houston State University down at Huntsville. Billy stayed home that first year, but after the Thanksgiving break of her sophomore year, Jimmie loaded Billy in her horse trailer and Billy went to college.

Green though he was under her hand, Jimmie knew from the start that this time a young horsewoman's dream had come true. In their first real test in a large competitive field, the Women's Invitational Barrel Race held in conjunction with the Fort Worth Fat Stock Show and Rodeo held in January 1972, Jimmie and Billy placed twice out of four runs. And she hadn't really let him go all out! Time built trust. The rest is intimated in record book history: $150,000 worth of winnings receipts, the prize saddles, the trophies and the buckles that filled the Gibbs living room.

When Doug Van Zandt and his technician pulled out onto the long highway home to Montana, a deep sadness rode between them. "I began questioning my own abilities and my own self," he reflected, three years later. "When you give it really all you have and you lose the ballgame, sometimes you just can't justify it.

"I couldn't really pin it down. I knew in reality that we were fighting a losing battle, but you know, that's the name of the game. These are the ones that are fun to win.

"And horrid to lose.

"If I had just been able to sit down and pinpoint it and say, 'This is the reason I didn't!' But I couldn't do that. There were so many gaps and so many variables.

"I found myself going back to CSU and doing a lot of research work and study. I truly believe that I have a great deal to learn. There are holes in my knowledge; I fully recognize that.

"It took me a long time to justify the situation and accept it.

"Billy was one of a kind. In twenty years of practice, I've never seen an animal quite like him. I expect to practice for another good twenty years, and I really don't ever expect to see a relationship like Jimmie and Billy again. I really don't."

The practitioner mused over Billy's bloodlines. Flit Bar out of the mare Robin Hood Price. He was a great grandson of Three Bars, a grandson of Sugar Bars, and then he was a grandson of Leo and a great grandson of Flying Bob, and a great grandson of Oklahoma Star. He judged you probably could pick class horses by genealogies, but when it really came to the outstanding individuals . . .

Also, Billy was well put together, a fair balance of speed and maneuverability. Yet the horse doctor had seen animals on the track and around the rodeo arena that were put together a lot better, anatomically. Many others that probably had more innate ability.

"But I've never seen a horse that was that supremely cool and competitive.

"It was a privilege to work on a horse like that, and I know that Jimmie treasured the many moments and times, and days and nights . . . the countless hours that she hauled that old guy around. For Jimmie to have raised him and have had him a part of her life . . . I'm sure as the years go on she'll be able to look back and see the influence that old horse had on her life. It's amazing. It truly is amazing!"

Since they laid Billy to rest beside old Bill under the oak tree on the hill, Jimmie Gibbs *has* lived out the legacy left her by those two grand veterans. In October of that year Jimmie married Bud Munroe, and together they have continued to go for the rodeo gold. In competition, Jimmie stands in a rare class of professional horsewomen, perennially among the top finalists in the world of women's professional rodeo; passing her knowledge on to the young colts who have followed Billy under her hand.

In her rodeo life, Jimmie Gibbs Munroe has given back to the sport as much as she has received. During her presidency, she has seen the Girls Rodeo Association become the Women's Professional Rodeo Association in name, in stature among rodeo events, and in the professionalism within the ranks of those she represents. A relatively new event, the barrel race has come into equal standing with the standard PRCA men's competitive events. And with equal pay, at the majority of the PRCA-sanctioned shows. Sponsorships have contributed to the women's event to bring its excitement and competitive spirit into the public eye. In 1983, the *Rodeo Sports News Annual* will include the women's barrel race competition for the first time in its coverage of the National Finals Rodeo.

Looking back in remembrance of Billy, Jimmie said, "I feel I was just fortunate that I had him, he was such a great horse. If I could have picked the time in my life that I could have had him, that would have been the time that I would have wanted him. I was able to compete on him in college and in my first few years as a professional, rather than when I was really young, in high school or in junior rodeo. Then, maybe then, you don't realized quite as much what you do have.

"Too, if I had come to have Billy when I was younger, I might have been tempted to skip the junior rodeos to run with him against his class of competition. I'm glad I was able to come up through junior rodeos and high school competition with my friends and my peers, then to have Billy when I was ready to graduate into the competition that college and professional rodeo had to offer.

"The only thing that I can look back on now and see, which I didn't see at the time, is that I never watched him grow old. When I lost him, he was running just as well as he ever had.

"I wasn't ever faced with the problem of knowing when to retire him. He was reaching the age when most horses slow down, and I worried whether I would know when it was time to let him go, and go on without him. He was such a beautiful animal; you hate to think about watching them grow old. But that was something I never had to confront with Billy. When he reached his pinnacle, he passed on."

At the Valley Veterinary Service, Dr. Van Zandt continues to work with equine medicine, physician in residence for the horse world—from the hobby horses of young girls in pigtails to the champions of the track and rodeo circuit. In thinking on the experience of Jimmie and Billy, the sweetness of the memories and the sadness of the loss that a rodeo girl inevitably must one day come to face, his thoughts turned inward.

"In rodeo," he began slowly, carefully choosing his words, "the hype, and the things that we see and the things that basically we daily read have precious little to do with it. That's kind of the frosting on the cake. The true substance behind it has a lot to do with . . . hard work, and competition. Just good solid healthy competitive spirit. And a lot of heart . . . and heartache.

"There are individual contests in life that are epitomized in rodeo, and experienced day to day.

"If anyone along the line ever is fortunate enough to come up with an experience like that, an animal like Billy comes but once in a lifetime. It shapes your whole life.

"Enjoy it while you can. Indeed so."

A Tale of Two Toros, I

Nothing much happens in Gladewater, Texas, ten miles of piney woods, pasture, and oilfields north of Interstate 20 and its endless procession of semi-trucks plying their way between Shreveport and Dallas. Talk along the main street revolves around those issues vital to any east Texas oil patch community: the weather, oilfield activity, livestock prices in Fort Worth, politics in Dallas. And that's the way folks like it; why they live here, raise their kids here.

But each year in June, when the oppressively hot air hangs muggy in the hollows, Gladewater relives in colorful pageantry the wild and woolly epic of its Texas frontier legacy, when the rodeo comes to town.

Wending their way off the interstate exchange, past a patchwork of oak, hickory, and pine, and the ever present oil derrick skeletons with their pump jacks bobbing like mechanical grasshoppers, and into the fairgrounds in the hollow at the edge of town came the semi-trailer trucks, BILLY MINICK RODEO COMPANY emblazoned down their sides, each bearing a jostling load of roping calves, *corriente* steers, saddle broncs, bareback horses, or rodeo bucking bulls.

Bulls of every exotic variety imaginable. Black Angus. White Charolais. Brightly splotched Mexican crosses. Wicked, hump-backed Brahmas. Crowding through the trailer tailgate. Clattering down the wooden ramp to mill in pens of discarded oilwell casing and sucker rod.

One bull stood out from all the others, lordly king of the macabre. Ominous in his ill-fitting coat of alkali grey, huge charcoal hump, upturned horns, and evil death-mask face. V61 was his name, after the brand scorched on the left side of his heavily muscled back. Eighteen hundred pounds of agility rippled pantherlike beneath his loosely clinging hide. Four hundred and fifty riders had tried him; four hundred and fifty had failed.

Nine years before, V61 had been an orphan bullcalf, bottle-weaned by a family of migrant farm workers, exuberant in his cantankerousness. At three he went through the stockyards in a line headed for the cannery, saved only by a stock-wise rancher who recognized in his snuffy disposition the potential for the rodeo arena.

Rudy Vela gambled twenty-two cents a pound on his hunch. But the Brahma he branded V61 didn't disappoint him. Even the dummy rider Vela tied to his back couldn't stay with the powerful leaps and vertical headstands of the explosive bull. Nor could the Texas amateurs who had the misfortune of drawing V61 out of the Sloan Willians string where the bull next resided. Nor could the bullriders of the International Rodeo Association circuit. Nor could the professionals of the RCA since Billy Minick had picked him up two years before. Not even at the National Finals.

V61 was the 1970 Bull of the Year. Superstar of the Billy Minick string.

Rodeo judges Dickey Cox and Ed Galemba conducted the drawing, randomly assigning the stock to the list of cowboys entered in the Gladewater Roundup Rodeo. Dickey Cox smiled

John Quintana and V61, Fort Worth 1972. *Photo by Bruce McShan, courtesy John Quintana*

wanly as the paper marked "V61" was pulled from the hat. Dickey had drawn the bull in the sixth go-round of the 1970 National Finals the previous December. The sixth was the final go-round for Dickey Cox. With the first mighty leap from the gate, V61 had jerked Cox back, stretched him out, suspended him from his riding arm. Then, with the steep pitch in landing, the bull flung Dickey forward, his face smashing against the animal's skull. Nine days he had lain in the Oklahoma City hospital getting his face put back together. Dickey Cox pitied the rider whose name was called: John Quintana.

Johnny Quintana was twenty-four, a sincere and unpretentious bull rider with athletic quickness belying his 175 pounds and five-feet, ten-inch frame—towering in comparison to the majority of his competitors. In an era of bullriding strongmen who mashed their feet and puffed out their chests to make an ugly face in an eight-second battle of strength, John's style contrasted as markedly as did his height—constantly shifting his body, hustling with his feet, counterbalancing with his free arm. Twice the lanky Oregonian's agility had carried him to the National Finals, ranking fourteenth in the world among professional bullriders. But this year he was riding better than he ever had. Fresh from a fourth-place split the previous week at the lucrative Fort Smith, Arkansas rodeo, Quintana came to Gladewater with a positive attitude, an emotional high. He knew he had drawn to win. There was no question in his mind that this night V61 would be conquered. By Johnny Quintana.

Johnny had caught a ride down from Dallas with two Wyoming bronc riders, John Holman and John Forbes. Dragging his war bag from the jumble in Holman's car trunk, he programmed his mind with every move he'd seen V61 make, and every strategy, every movement he would have to marshal to checkmate the Bull of the Year. For V61 was an intelligent, unpredictable animal, cunningly directing his tiger movements to advantage, sensing the rider's weakness, and shifting his weight within his rippling hide to shuck the unsuspecting. But most of all it was the muscle-tearing power that John knew he had to handle.

And when the gate opened there would be time only for reaction. For programmed reflex.

John Quintana's equipment was designed to match his scrambling style of riding. With the shuffling action of his feet, often in combination with squeezing pressure with his knees, Quintana didn't lock his ankles with toes pointed to the points of the compass as did the riders who tried to maintain a steady spurhold. His two-inch shank spurs were canted inward to where the rowels could touch a surface parallel with the inner bootheel band. Leather straps over the arch and under the front of the bootheel bound his spurs to his boots with just the slightest give under tension. His large five-point rowels also were designed to keep him conscious of his feet, rotating with each grasp nearly ninety degrees before catching on the lock screw pinned through the shank, reducing the power transmitted by the bull. Keeping the cowboy hustling for a spurhold.

Like the bareback riders, John buckled tie-down straps about his ankles to keep from spurring his boots from his feet. His chaps too were on the order of a bareback rider's, of medium-weight leather to protect his legs from bruising blows and slashing hooves. His riding glove, in an era when goatskin was unavailable, was of elkhide—a heavy leather, even a little mushy in his grip. It took rosin well and would bubble up at the base of his fingers to roll over the bullrope handle when his fist was clenched. A leather thong would wrap around his wrist to bind the glove to his hand.

One end of John's ten-foot manila hemp bullrope was formed into an adjustable loop, held by a common bowline knot. A heavy metal rectangular bell with a cast iron clapper was suspended from the loop by a leather strap. The clapper's incessant clanging through a ride was thought to goad the bull to more frenzied pitching, but the heavy bell's primary function was to drag the rope free of the animal after the rider had departed, either by choice or at the bull's behest.

The remaining six-foot length of the hemp had been unraveled and woven with a five-plait braid. At the base of the braid an added handhold loop was braided into the rope with four inches or "five fingers" of slack vertically between it and the bullrope body. Rather than binding his hand to the bull when the rope was tightened, this slack allowed more freedom of hand movement, absorbing much of the tremendous jerking power of a bull such as V61. Added to the handle was a plait of whang leather, plaited on an angle forward to the right and parallel with the fingers of Quintana's left hand grip. Where hemp alone would compress and curl, the leather gave strength and body to the handhold braid, lying flat in John's grip.

A length of 1/8-inch nylon cord also was braided into the "wear strip" where the braided tail threaded through the bell loop in securing the bullrope about the animal's girth. Should the hemp give way under strain, the high tensile strength nylon would hold the rope together.

As the bulls were being driven into the bucking chutes, John secured his bullrope on the fence behind the chutes. Then, drawing a wire brush from his bag, he scraped away the caked rosin built up on the braided tail. With small chunks of rosin cradled in the palm of his glove, he gripped the rope tail below the wear strip, slowly pulling it through his grasp to coat the hemp strands and his glove with the sticky, friction-heated residue. He repeated the process with the handhold loop.

Tucking his warm glove in the belt of his chaps, John untied his rope from the fence. V61 was deeper in the chest than the last bull he had drawn. The rope was adjusted too short to fit the eighteen-hundred-pound Brahma. From the bell loop Quintana fed the rope back into the bowline knot, retrieving the slack at the loose end leading to his handhold.

Climbing the left-hand delivery chute gate, John slid the loop end of the rope over V61's back until the bell struck the ground behind the bull's right front leg. V61 pawed the hard-packed earth, a rumble rolling deep from his throat. John peered through the gate slats, fishing with a wire hook to snag the bullrope loop in front of the strap of the metal bell. Threading the braided tail toward him through the loop, Quintana pulled up the slack and tucked the loose tail under his handhold.

The rodeo clowns, barrelman Tom Lucia and veteran bull-fighter George Doak, rolled their barrel front-and-center before the chutes, bantering one-liners with the announcer to the peal of laughter from the 5,500 spectators jam-packed around the small arena. Billy Minick worked his way down the line, knotting sheepskin-padded ropes about the bulls' flanks, each in turn. John Quintana briskly warmed up with isometrics and contortions to stretch tense muscles, especially those of the groin; then climbed over the chute to squeeze his legs down alongside the bull filling the compartment. Gingerly he felt for a foothold on the boards below, keeping his toes turned inward to avoid touching the volatile V61's sides with his spur rowels. With both hands he rolled the rope back and forth behind the bull's hump to center the bell beneath. He aligned the butt of the handhold over V61's backbone and shoved the rope forward against the hump.

With bronc rider John Holman standing on the gate, lifting upward on the loose tail of his rope Quintana drew on his elk-skin glove, working each finger deep before wrapping the leather thong about his wrist. Then, calling to Holman for tension on the rope, he worked his gloved left hand up and down the taut tail, the friction of his grip again heating the rosin to stickiness.

From the chute ahead a bull and rider exploded into the arena to the rousing cheers of the enthusiastic crowd. The next bull out would be V61. John glanced down to see the end of his bell loop properly aligned at the bull's left elbow. Then, calling to Holman for slack, he began pulling folds of loose hide forward under the bullrope.

The ride in the arena was over. The rider was safe on the ground, the bull diving with ruffled dignity through the open catch-pen gate, with bullfighter George Doak whopping at his heels. From their perches on the arena fence, the judges bent to scribble their scores. A hush fell over the crowd as the announcer reviewed the credentials of V61, the unridden Bull of the Year. Grinning with pride Billy Minick bent over his star to make a last-minute adjustment to the flank strap, urging the rider to "Hurry every chance you get."

With palm turned upward, John Quintana pushed his gloved hand into the handhold, deep against the base of his thumb, snugging his little finger along the handhold base centered over V61's backbone. Calling again for tension on the rope, he tugged the handle back from the hump. The rope settled to a natural position at the base of V61's broad trapezius neck muscle.

John Holman pulled the rope snug, almost tight. With his fingers Holman pinched the tail tightly against the rope just above its turn through the bell loop, preventing it from slipping slack. Quintana laid the braided tail over the handle in his palm. The loose end was wrapped around the back of his hand, not tightly but with a "two finger" wide clearance or "bubble" out from his glove. The bubble would save the rider's hand from being squeezed, garrotelike, with the expansion of V61's chest when he blew from the chute.

The loose end was twisted to lie across John's palm on edge between his fingers and the handhold. John closed his fingers over the rosined handle and two thicknesses of tail wrap, then locked his thumb across the fist. The remaining tail, John's ripcord, lay forward over V61's hump, in close reach.

The hush hung heavy over the Gladewater arena. The crowd leaned forward with bated breath, craning their necks for a better view, unblinking for fear of missing this climactic moment. Johnny Quintana scooted up against his clenched fist, tucked his riding arm with elbow bent close against his side, and leaned forward over V61's tense back, his ice blue eyes sighting fiercely down the Brahma's neck. He gulped the soggy night air deep into his chest. Gritted his teeth. Tucked his chin. Called for the gate. And drove his spurs ahead of the bullrope.

V61 whirled, hooking the half-open gate with his massive head. Slamming it back. Sending the gate man reeling. The bull uncoiled, blowing into the arena in a spectacular leap, his hind legs tucked under him. Quintana was whipped back against his arm, straining to keep his elbow bent, to keep from being snatched by the bull's tremendous thrust. He mashed his heels like never before, helpless to stop the unbelievable power from squirting forward beneath the loose hide. He heaved upward on the bullrope. Grimacing. Squeezing the handhold to keep it from wrenching from his grasp.

At the peak of his dive, V61's head plunged downward between his legs. The east Texas soil rushed upward, meeting the shocked rider's stare where only a split moment before the bulging neck and a rack of horns had commanded his view over the ugly hump. With all his might the rider flung his free arm back over his head, counterbalancing in anticipation of the forward-slamming thrust.

Fifteen feet beyond the gate V61 landed headfirst, then jack-knifed, stretched out, his rear quarters kicking over his head. The g's of force instantaneously reversed their field. Quintana's feet popped forward. His knees jammed into the hump. His pelvis slammed against his gloved fist. His knuckles rammed against the bullrope pad in a complete handstand on his riding arm. The Brahma's loose hide rolled forward in combers, bunching up against the pylons of his shoulders. Texas dust and dandruff rose in turbulent clouds from his hide. He tossed his head, again filling the rider's vision with his wicked upturned horns. Saliva ribboned from his blunt muzzle.

V61's rear quarters recoiled, driving forward beneath him, reaching for the earth. Quintana sprang forward, his feet hustling to clutch the hide ahead of his rope. He threw his free arm forward with elbow bent, his hand level with his face, pointing straight ahead. He jumped out over his rope. Against the towering hump. Ahead of the onslaught.

V61 again shot upward, passing through the death-grip of Quintana's legs. John's neck contracted. He strained forward against the thrust, fighting to keep his shock-absorbing elbow bent; dissipating the whiplash racing up his spine.

The Brahma slung his powerful neck to the right, twisting within his hide in midair, dropping his right shoulder, turning back into the momentum of his hind quarters. His head vanished beneath the hump. John whipped his free arm back behind his head with an upward sweep and leaned into the whirl, away from his riding arm, bearing the length of his right leg tightly against the bull. Hauling in on his handhold he squirmed to stay up with the bullrope, jockeying his buttocks against the right side of V61's spine, inside the spin, safe from the snatching centrifugal force. His left leg slashed forward, reaching for the spurhold he had lost.

V61 hit the ground, walking on his front legs to keep from being thrown over by the momentum of his arching rear quarters. His motion lurched the rider first to the left, then to the right, toward the "well" of the spin. Once more John threw his torso back with the lever of his free arm and absorbed the muscle-tearing impact, ramming his knees against the hump. Then scrambling for a spurhold, once more throwing himself forward with his free arm.

V61 pivoted in a flash, whipping upward, ever to the right and away from Quintana's riding hand. John clamped his legs against the lurch, squeezing the ribs rippling past beneath loose skin. The bull's hide was rolling, pitching the rider to the outside of the whirl, into his riding arm. John's free arm arched high behind his head, rotating in its socket to throw his torso back, catching up to the whirl of the animal. He jockeyed his buttocks up against his rope, feathering his pull against the rope handle, a pull that could compound the centrifugal force jerking him to the outside of the spin. He threw his left foot forward, chasing the accelerating animal's center of gravity.

The Brahma's hind quarters rolled to kick vertically in delayed action after his landing. Once more he stumbled forward to catch his balance, crossing his front legs in his rotation, slinging his mighty neck, nearly hooking John's right leg. Then once more Quintana jumped ahead of the bull's drive, throwing his free arm forward, elbow bent in an "L."

V61's spine rolled. Half a ton of beef smashed rear hooves like piledrivers into the loose dirt, launching his front end whirling upward to the right in lurching gyration. Rolling in the air. Twisting within his ill-fitting coat. Falling behind the momentum of hind quarters sweeping high in the night air. Sideslipping beneath the straining rider. Plummeting in a vertical headstand. Kicking with heels in delayed action. Staggering. A tower of beef collapsing. Crashing. Pile-driver hooves slamming back to the launching pad.

Quintana's face was drawn with the torque. Every ounce of his body strained against the forces blowing him behind V61's thrust, tearing him to the outside of the spin, ripping his feet back, his torso ahead, then slamming him against the shoulder hump. His right leg squeezed the bull tightly inside the spin. His free arm whipped upward, behind his head, throwing his body back. Twisting his torso in clockwise gyration. Countering his body reflexes in crucially timed cadence to catch up to the Brahma's terrific diving whirl. Knifing his left leg forward. Hustling against tremendous centrifugal force. And constantly jockeying, squirming his buttocks close to the bullrope.

The crowd was on its feet screaming like banshees. John's ears failed to catch the rasp of the buzzer in the midst the bedlam about him. Once, twice more after the Klaxon, V61 whirled in lurching, high-diving rotation to the right. Quintana was weakening. The cadence of his own gyration fell behind the bull's momentum. His left spur now clutched determinedly but futilely against the creeping hide. His balance tilted. His seat slowly slid away from the bull's backbone, sinking into the whirlpool. With abandon his flung his free arm, stretching behind his head, momentarily lifting his body away from the incessant tug of gravity. From the pounding hooves.

Now V61 was in full control. With his aerial thrust he could snatch Quintana's riding arm straight, to whiplash him forward in descent, blowing his feet behind, propelling his head forward to smash against the wicked horned skull.

Worse, the rider was in danger of hanging up to the bull. With a headfirst flip into the well, opposite his riding arm, his gloved hand would twist in the bullrope, the handle pinching his knuckles against V61's back, locking the tailwrap about his fist. Leaving him helpless to escape the battering horns and trampling hooves.

Bullfighter George Doak edged forward, ready to charge in. To intercept the whirling circle. To distract V61. To save John Quintana.

On the brink of disaster, Quintana released his grip, popping his fingers straight. Simultaneously he jerked his gloved hand free of the wrap and kicked his left leg over the hump in a barrel roll away from his riding arm. He landed on both feet in a crouch, within the whirlpool of the bull's spin. Vulnerable to attack.

V61 twisted violently, Changed leads. Swung his muscular

neck. Disdainfully. Away from the human target churning through the deep soft dirt toward the safety of the fence. V61 was not a headhunter; it was beneath his dignity. His work was finished.

George Doak's assistance was unnecessary.

The crowd was wild. Croaking hoarse cheers. Whistling. Strangers thumping each other on the back. Incredulous in this magnificent moment. John Quintana stared numbly at the pandemonium about him. Slowly the realization sank in. Shock turned to elation. He had ridden V61. He had conquered the unconquerable. The Bull of the Year.

Ed Galemba stared overwhelmed at his judging sheet, wishing he could give the book to the now grinning bullrider draped against the fence. Resolutely, he took his pencil in hand and made his marking: 24 each to the bull and rider, as close to perfection as he'd ever dreamed he'd see. The scorekeeper ran to Dickey Cox for his score: 23 for the rider, 23 for the bull, higher than Cox had ever scored in his life. Or ever hoped to.

The announcer shouted the verdict over the noise of the celebrating spectators. Johnny Quintana and V61 had marked a 94, the highest score in any riding event in the entire history of rodeo. Right there in Gladewater, Texas.

A Tale of Two Toros, II

John Quintana's riding event record fell the next year. At Albuquerque, on a rapid-fire spinning Charolais-Dairy cross bull known as Double Ought, of the Beutler Brothers and Cervi string, the rookie bull rider Jack Himes kicked out a score of 95. The animal had been ridden impressively but once before, by Johnny Quintana.

Controversial in its precedence was the marking of 50 points awarded Himes by judge Ron Taylor. Never before had a ride received the ultimate, perfection. Taylor's decision shattered rodeo tradition, and set a standard for striving never before thought possible.

At Las Vegas in 1974 John Quintana drew Cervi's notorious General Isomo. The lean Brahma jumped into counterclockwise reversals at the gate, whirling into John's riding arm in mock mirror image of V61's Gladewater trip, with his phenomenal acceleration generating less muscle-tearing power but much greater centrifugal pull. Charging with rapid cadence born of reflex, John leaned into the spin and flung his free arm "in the back door" behind his head in precision counterbalance to the centrifugal force dragging him outside the whirl, away

Don Gay and Oscar, NFR 1977. *Photo by Dave Allen*

from his handhold. Through eleven, perhaps twelve revolutions, General Isomo tucked into the eight-second contest with Quintana scrambling to top the lurching gyrations. When the dust had settled the tally was 96, a record that would stand for over three years.

In 1972 John Quintana claimed the world diadem. The year 1972 also saw the professional debut of a self-assured young Texan, Don Gay. Number two scion of the all-rodeo Neal Gay family of Mesquite, Don ascended to the eighth slot in world standings and stole the show at the National Finals with a commanding 89 performance on Billy Minick's Number 45 to win the ninth go-round. It was the highest mark of the rodeo and the beginning of a bullriding dynasty.

Four ingredients catalyzed to make Don Gay perhaps the greatest bull rider ever: superb physical condition; training in

bull-riding fundamentals; constant practice; and a positive, no, *commanding* mental attitude.

"Tough like a compact grizzly bear," at five feet, six inches and 140 pounds, Gay used his compactness to advantage: "You have less body weight to contend with and your reaction time is faster. That automatically tells you it's reaction time that counts in bullriding, because no human being is going to be stronger than a 2,000-pound bull. A bullrider doesn't ride with strength."

From an early age Don Gay honed his skills methodically, developing balance to instinctive reaction first in the topsy-turvy world of kids' calf riding, then on the rafter-backed corriente steers. At fifteen he took on the tryout bulls for his daddy's Mesquite Rodeo string.

With his older brother Pete, the aspiring young rider traveled to Henryetta, Oklahoma, and the rodeo school of their daddy's one-time travel mate and business partner, world all-around champion Jim Shoulders.

On the principle that walking first must be mastered before running could be achieved, Shoulders carefully matched bulls to each rider's abilities, wisely building confidence before graduating them to animals of greater speed or power. Under the master's critical eye, Don Gay put together the moves essential in handling the pattern variations of the bucking bull. Returning home he practiced, constantly working out the fundamentals on the slower and less powerful bulls of the Mesquite string until moves were performed automatically, in reflex action and on cue from the animals' movements. Basic maneuvers were repeated literally hundreds of times before Don hit the professional circuit full time after finishing high school.

The influence of Don Gay's traveling companions during his first year "going down the road" was paramount in shaping his destiny. From men such as 1970 world champion bull rider Gary Leffew, Gay learned to experience the power of positive thinking and the success mechanisms of psychocybernetics, a philosophy viewing the physical subconscious brain and nervous system network as a complex goal-striving servomechanism operating purposefully at the command of the mind. Don became indoctrinated in the belief that anything was possible, that his "self-image" set the boundaries of individual accomplishment. He had only to expand his self-image to expand his "area of the possible."

"Every obstacle is only a weakness in your mind," Leffew counseled. "Be great because it is in you, if you only believe."

Like learning to walk, or finding your mouth in feeding yourself, once a correct response pattern has been accomplished it is stored in "memory" for future use, duplicating successful responses in future trials without consciously issuing orders to individual muscles, nor calculating just how much muscle contraction is needed. Once programmed, his built-in servomechanism could function subconsciously, reacting to stimuli from the bull, automatically adjusting his balance—a success mechanism accomplishing his goals. Don had only to create "that winning feeling," then relax his conscious controls to keep from jamming the machinery he had programmed for success.

Don Gay attacked the world of bull riding aggressively, with youthful exuberance, a generous helping of self-esteem, and an unswerving faith in a God who created man in His image. His daring, hurry-scurry riding, and ability to perform the "impossible" bullride became his trademark. In 1973 he lost the world title to fellow Texan Bobby Steiner—the man who perfected the stylish sweep of the free hand—in the very last go-round of the National Finals. But in 1974 he claimed the crown with authority, wildly spurring an NFR-record 94 on Billy Minick's Tiger, Bull of the Year. In 1975, traveling to a phenomenal 171 rodeos and winning nearly $35,000, he topped his own earnings record in the event. He picked up $3,400 at Denver; $2,300 at Edmonton; $2,000 each at Dallas and San Francisco; and a whopping $3,950 at the National Finals, despite hanging up to Walter of the Reg Kesler string in the ninth go-round, to a nation-wide television audience. In a cliff-hanger of a title race with Randy Magers in 1976, Gay clinched the crown in the last go-round with a spectacular exhibition of reckless aggression on Joe Kelsey's high leaping Red One. His 95 score beat his own National Finals Rodeo record.

Rising to stardom in a rodeo career markedly counterpoint to that of bull rider Don Gay was the small whirling dervish of the Rodeo Stock Contractors (RSC) string, Number 16, Oscar. Bred for the rodeo arena, he was the Brahma-cross offspring of an RSC bucking bull, raised at contractor Bob Cook's Clements, California spread. Oscar was V61 in miniature, straight from Hades with an ash-gray coat, a charred shoulder cloak, smudged eyes, and the swept-back horns of Lucifer. He tipped the scales at only 1,150 pounds but rapidly gained notoriety as unrideable with a spectacular high kick and phenomenal speed, handily wrapping a dozen counterclockwise reversals into an eight-second display. A hundred-RPM antlered cartwheel.

By the age of six he had been covered but once in 156 tries, and that not impressively. John Davis had been whipped to the outside of the tight spin, clinging out of control at the whistle. Mexico's premier Charro had wagered $10,000 on his ability to handle the bull for five seconds, with a two-hand grip. He lasted but two.

Then, at the 1974 National Finals Jerome Robinson mashed his spurs and pumped his free arm "in the back door" behind his head to rack up a respectable 86. The unrideable Oscar finally had been conquered.

But it was Don Gay, not Jerome Robinson who stole the show that year, with his frenzied scrambling to set the NFR record on Tiger. Oscar would have to wait for his accolades.

That opportunity didn't come until three years later, at the close of the 1977 season, in San Francisco's famed Cow Palace. It was the final performance of the final rodeo of the year. Oscar stood in the last left-hand delivery chute, the final bull of the evening. His rider, Don Gay.

Bob Tallman announced the rodeo, charging the atmosphere with excitement, piquing a sellout crowd of 14,000 enthusiastic rodeo aficionados, in anticipation of the evening's climax.

Don Gay came to San Francisco with "that winning feeling." He was leading the world. He was healthy. He was even staying in his room at the Mission Bell Motel, where he always had stayed when he had won. He already had mastered Oscar, the previous year. He need only call forth the "memory," and put the servo in action.

Gay removed his bullrope, his fifth of the season, from its protective bag and unrolled it to amply "grease" the handle and tail in rosin, with friction against his goatskin glove, carefully avoiding getting rosin on the wear strip of the plaited rope tail. He shortened the rope to conform to the small barrel of Oscar's chest by feeding the length ahead of the handle into the bowline knot, and retrieving the slack to enlarge the bell loop. While many riders had evolved to a 9-plait bullrope, Don's rope was of a 7-plait fabrication, with lace leather woven into the handle, a soft pad beneath the handhold, and two heavy metal bells hanging from the bell loop. "A larger rope strains a bullrider more instead of him feeling loose. If a rider can keep his body moving and his feet moving, he is in better shape and his body does not take as much punishment."

Don placed his rope on Oscar in much the same manner as had John Quintana on V61. The bells were centered beneath Oscar's chest, and the end of the bell loop, where the tail threaded through, was aligned with the animal's left elbow. With longtime friend and champion bronc rider Monty Henson holding tension on the rope tail, he stood astraddle the narrow bull and drew the handhold back to a position at the base of the long neck muscle, with the butt of the handle centered over the animal's boney spine.

At the microphone Bob Tallman rattled off the many coups of the snakey Oscar, and played up Don Gay's reputation as master of impossible bulls, rider of the unrideable. Contractor Bob Cook stood at the back of the chute, motioning the clowns back. Like V61, Oscar was a bucking athlete, not a head hunter.

Judges Marty Backstrom and Ron Taylor—the same man who had awarded a 50-point score to Jack Himes in 1972—moved to positions on either side of the gate.

Don Gay secured his riding glove with a Velcro band of brother Pete's invention. With his little finger centered on Oscar's rafter-back, he called to Henson to snug the rope, with tension looser

than his competitors dared try. Don wanted all the body freedom available to adjust to Oscar's lightning moves.

Don laid the broad, mushy-woven tail across his palm, took a
loose wrap around the back of his hand, and again laid the
plaited tail across his palm, on edge against the base of his
fingers. Threading the tail out over the top of his little finger, as
a bronc rider grips the bucking rein, he closed his fingers with a
squeezing grip. He eased his seat forward against the rope. A
quick nod said, "Let's try the bull."

Don's feet jammed into the slab sides not a flash too soon.
Oscar boiled out of the chute, careening the gate out of his path.
He writhed in his loose hide to drop into the arena ninety degrees
to the left of his stance in the box. One leap straight. Then pivot-
ing sharply to the left, his outside leg striking out, crossing over
in the lead. Don jumped at the rope, wrenching with his wrist,
drawing his buttocks over into the whirl. Shuffling his feet in
hot pursuit. His free arm waving aloft, automatically adjusting
to the animal's shift. The rider's eye never wavered in concen-
tration on Oscar's neck and narrow shoulders.

Oscar hit the ground, simultaneously kicking over his head,
scooting Don forward into a handstand over his rope. Gay's
knees gripped the hump. His free arm curved forward, no sooner
than Oscar's hind hooves slammed to the ground, launching
bull and rider sharply upward, lurching to the left, into Don's
hand grip.

Gay's right leg knifed forward in a wide arc to clutch at the
animal's retreating shoulder. His free arm whipped behind his
head, counterbalancing "in the back door." His torso tilted awk-
wardly out over the vortex of the swirl. Oscar turned back catlike in midair, ducking back under the drive of his hind quarters,
tightening the spin, jerking Gay upright.

Don's wrist pried on the rope, jockeying his buttocks back
over the uncoiling spine. It was like riding a writhing rail. Slip-

ping into the well. Whipping over to the outside with the centrifugal lurch.

Oscar hit his pace immediately in front of the chutes, a violent tornado churning the arena dirt in ever-tightening concentric circles. His rear quarters pumping like pistons, in each lightning leap. Slinging his neck. Leading with his outside foreleg. Whirling counterclockwise in midair. Turning back. Rolling within his loose hide. Tucking under the rear quarters. Tightening the circle. Accelerating the centrifugal force. Instantaneously landing, kicking over his head. Twisting his spine. Driving rear hooves forward to the earth. Faster and faster. Four, five six seven eightninteneleventwelve wraps.

Once Oscar swept beneath him to snatch his body upright, Don Gay jumped into the cadence of the maelstrom. Tapped off. Automatically reacting with programmed reflexes on cue. His free arm would drop into his vision ahead of each lunge, to whip sharply behind his head, checkmating the pulse of centrifugal g's. The cords of his neck stood out in relief. Tucking in his chin. Controlling his torso. Squeezing. Pumping the rope. Jumping from towline to handstand.

With Oscar's acceleration Don's cadence quickened. Throwing caution to the gale, he leapt at the whirlpool. Gapping his outside leg with reckless abandon. Exposing himself to the forces. Then gripping with his spurs. Pinching against Oscar's slab sides. Flexing his knees, his hip sockets. Dragging his rowels upward toward his gloved hand. Tilting into the spin. Squirming to keep his seat close to the bullrope. Flinging his free arm behind his head. The shouts of the cowboys chanting in cadence to the psychocybernetics success machine.

At eight seconds the timer's thumb stabbed the ride into the history books. Don's ear caught the welcome buzzer rasping through the fog of swirling action. As Oscar lunged, he grabbed the loose tail of the bullrope with his free hand, ripping the wrap from his grip. His gloved fingers snapped straight, slipping free of the bullrope. He kicked his legs out from the bull. The ascent of Oscar's rear quarters lifted the rider clear of the storm. Don lit on his hands and knees, sprinting for the safety of the chute. And the standing ovation of fourteen thousand cheering people.

John Quintana's record fell that night. Don Gay's ride on Oscar was marked a 97. Marty Backstrom tallied 47 points. Ron Taylor, torching anew the controversial institutions of rodeo tradition, tributed 50. Again, he'd seen the best.

Fate rematched Don Gay and the infamous Oscar one month later, at the National Finals. Seven seconds into the set-to, Oscar jumped out of his spin, snaking back to the right. Psycho-cybernetics hit the dirt.

Epilogue; When You Get There

Some men search for silver;
Some men look for gold.
But you have found a treasure
Their pockets will never hold.

Some men look forever,
And still they never find;
They don't know that freedom
Is just a state of mind.

Chris LeDoux

John Hutson doesn't wear a big gold World Champion Cowboy belt buckle. He isn't tall or muscular. Not a man to make a striking impression, really, from a distance.

But John Hutson is really something. Someone anyone would be proud to know.

He said, "The only thing you have when you get there is what you sent on ahead."

He said it again. "The only thing you have when you get there is what you sent on ahead."

"Calvin Bohleen," he said. "Calvin Bohleen is what I mean."

Calvin Bohleen is a cowboy. By any cowboy measure. He's tall, and big, and he has several gold belt buckles. He also is a successful businessman, a cattle buyer with a reputation of respect.

Cal Bohleen also is an extraordinary western artist; extraordinarily good, in a field as crowded as the Cheyenne Frontier Days bull riding.

The business card in his left shirt pocket says: "Calvin R. Bohleen Cattle & Horses Bought, Sold, Traded & Painted."

Calvin Bohleen has another paper, from the United States Jaycees. It says that Calvin Bohleen is among the top ten outstanding men in America.

John Hutson has admiration for Calvin Bohleen. But these are not the reasons. It is because, John Hutson said, "the only thing you have when you get there is what you sent on ahead."

That's why John Hutson is high on Calvin Bohleen.

Cal Bohleen entered the 1972 rodeo at Prairie Du Chien, Wisconsin, over Labor Day weekend. When Cal's steer came out into the arena, with him thundering alongside, his hazer pounding the turf on the other side, something went wrong. Calvin Bohleen of Wilsall, Montana, broke his neck.

Cal was transferred by air ambulance to the Craig Rehabilitation Center in Denver. From September 1972 through January of the next year, he was flat on his back, a respirator doing his breathing for him.

Calvin Bohleen was paralyzed from the neck down.

Cal Bohleen is still paralyzed. But all that occurred *before* he was a successful cattle buyer, an extraordinary western artist, and recognized as one of the top ten outstanding men in America.

But Cal Bohleen has always been a man. That he was what

he was *before* his misfortunes is the reason he is the man he is *after* his misfortunes.

The only thing you have when you get there is what you sent on ahead.

Cal Bohleen put it another way. "I don't let it rule me," he told writer Rob Isham. "I don't spend time worrying about my recovery. When I die, I'm not going to be judged on whether I 'recovered' or not. I'm going to be judged on how I handled the handicap.

"People out West expect you to measure up. I can't stand to lose. I like to succeed. I want to be better than the average run-of-the-mill guy.

"Rodeo gave me the best things that ever happened to me. Regardless of the accident."

John Hutson and I talked about rodeo. For twenty-one years he has been an announcer. For twenty-three years he has served on the National High School Rodeo Association Board of Directors.

"My whole existence on the NHSRA Board has been to provide youth with the sport I love, and think they need.

"Not to build champions. But solid American citizens. Through the high school rodeo program.

"Your thanks are seeing young people succeed in life. Not just rodeo, sports, or horse activities.

"That's what it's all about. I do it for the kids, not as an ego trip."

John Hutson is doing the right things, for the right reasons.

"You know," he said, warming to his subject, "high school rodeo is the only sport or extracurricular activity where the kids are responsible for adults.

"Now, that's a neat twist.

"We adults spend so much time, and money, giving youth what we didn't have. We need, instead, to give them what we *did* have Responsibility. For themselves, as well as any livestock they have.

"The kids you read about on the front page of newspapers, kids in trouble, are less than 5 percent of youth today. There is a lot of *good* out there. Rodeo is an activity that can provide for release of natural youthful energy, a release that also carries a responsibility."

We talked of John Hutson's years as a rodeo announcer, and the high points in his career. He was the announcer behind the mike when Denny Flynn rode Bobby Steiner's Red Lightning—Number 11, the 1978 Bull of the Year—to the all-time highest score in bull-riding history, a 98.

"Everything told you, you were going to see something you had never seen before."

When the red-brindle bull with flat horns and anything but a flat, or straight, trajectory blew out of the chute, John Hutson said, "The bull did everything right. He had the drive, the power. The way he left the chute, and the speed he picked up as he went, was phenomenal.

"Denny became a part of the bull. I've never seen a man so much a part of an animal. It was like he was glued.

"Everything was right, as close to perfect as you can get.

"It was one of those exhilarating experiences of a lifetime. You see something like that . . . you won't forget it in your entire life."

John Hutson had one more thing to say: "You have to know Denny Flynn as a human being to really appreciate what happened that night."

Yes, Denny Flynn is another example: "The only thing you have when you get there is what you sent on ahead."

In 1975 at the Salt Lake City rodeo on July 23, Denny climbed down on a mediocre bull—"I think they were 60-some points on him in the first go-round"—a bull with "real high, sharp horns," as Denny put it later in discussing the ride with rodeo writer Barbara J. Brown.

"He wasn't hard to ride at all. I rode him easy.

"Just as I reached for the fence, he scooted out and ran me off my rope. I was straddling the flank, and my hand was still in the rope. The bull felt me on the flank, so he just kicked up and pole-vaulted me over my riding arm and down on his head.

"It happened so fast. The bull threw me back up in the air, and I did a complete flip and landed on the ground. I bounced up on my feet and ran back to the chutes.

"I knew I was hurt. I could feel it. It was numb, but there was a stinging feeling. There wasn't much pain, but I knew I was hurt real bad when I reached down and touched my intestines just hanging out."

The rest of the ordeal of Denny Flynn was related to Bob St. John by Denny and Randy Magers.

" 'I just thought the bull hit him with the horn,' recalled Magers. 'Then I saw the hole in his shirt. I helped him down off the fence and then pulled back his shirt. I like to fainted. Something was coming out, protruding.' "

"The bull's horn had shot up under Denny's rib cage," St. John explained in his book *On Down The Road*, "splitting his liver and stopping only a few inches from his heart. When the horn was jerked back out, as quickly as it had gone in, some of his intestines came with it.

"Denny Flynn, his face grayish white, thought he was dying. 'I was scared, I guess about in shock, but I thought it was over. My mind was racing back on my life, different things I wished I'd done.' Attendants from the ambulance wanted him to lie down. But whenever he did, the fluid would move into his lungs and he couldn't breathe. 'I kept getting up,' recalled Denny. 'When I stood up I could breathe. I never lost consciousness. I was afraid to close my eyes because I thought I'd die.'

" 'I kept him talking all the time,' said Magers. 'I was afraid if he stopped talking, he'd pass out and die. I thought he was a goner.'

"Talking: 'Hey, I feel like I'm bleeding inside. Hey.'

" 'It don't look too bad, Denny. Just relax. We'll be at the hospital soon. Just relax.'

" 'Bad. It looks bad.'

" 'No, it don't, Denny. No, it don't. It'll be all right. Just relax as much as you can. We're about there.'

"They got him to the hospital and rushed him into surgery," St. John continued. "Before they put him to sleep, the doctor told him he would be fine and Denny believed him. 'That's the first time I thought I'd make it,' he said."

The days following his accident for Denny Flynn were unforgettable. Intensive care; fear of infection. Fear of fear itself. It was a time of looking over what he had sent on ahead.

It was all there when he got there.

" 'The doctor told me to be prepared for a long stay in the hospital,' he said. 'We figured three, four weeks. But I was out of intensive care in three days, and in three more I was out of the hospital. They let me go home. 'Course, the tubes were still in me and I felt a little shaky.'

" 'Soon as I was able to move around pretty good and could get out the tubes, I went out and got on this ol' muley bull I had. It made me feel a little uneasy, but I pretty well knew what that bull would do. I was back on the rodeo circuit at Madison Square Garden in October. I placed, and then I won second in Memphis.'

" 'I saw that bull and almost turned out. But, you know, you got to do it sooner or later. I was scared to death when I got on, but then I forgot what had happened before.' "

St. John continues: "Denny Flynn was fifteenth in bull riding, the last spot in which he could make the Finals. By the Finals,

Don Gay had already cinched his second straight bull riding championship, but Denny didn't care. 'Well, I'm just happy to make it,' he said. 'You qualify and there's no way you miss it. No way.' "

At the National Finals, four months after he had been gored in the chest, Denny Flynn won the 1975 NFR bull-riding championship.

"If you'd talked to the people who took him to the hospital and stayed with him and then saw this man in sixty days come back and ride again and come to the National Finals Rodeo and be leading in bullriding," Sandy Kirby told St. John, "you'd know what the professional rodeo athlete is all about."

Denny Flynn was back, and riding better than he ever had before. "Without a doubt," the *Rodeo Sports News Annual* reported of his third-place finish in 1977 behind Don Gay and Randy Magers, "Denny Flynn is one of the truly 'rank bull' riders around."

In 1978, Denny went into the National Finals in second place, within reach of overtaking Don Gay for the world title. He placed in only three go-rounds and had to turn out his eleventh bull due to injury.

In 1979, at Palestine, Illinois, Denny was given his opportunity to fulfill his promise as a rider of rank bulls. He had drawn Red Lightning, the Bull of the Year.

Bobby Steiner had purchased the bull from Cecil and Alfred Hill of Oak Hills, Texas, on a tip from Andy Carey. "The bull only weighed 900 pounds," he told writer Ed Knocke.

"He finally came into his own at Kansas City in 1977. I had a clown bait the bull and turn him back. Now he turns back on his own."

"He's not unrideable," Steiner said in May 1979. "He's been out of the chute 49 times this year and he's been ridden six. His score is 1–1 with Don Gay, Denny Flynn, Butch Kirby and 2–2 with Mike Bandy.

125

"He's an honest bull with a lot of action," Steiner added of his red-brindle bucking star now weighing 1650 pounds. "The buckingest bull I've ever owned. He spins right in the gate, and has three ways of going.

"Red is not an impossible bull, but he's right next to it. And he's not a real fighting bull, though he's snorty and he will hit you if you're in his way after he's thrown a rider."

Steiner named his bull in response to a suggestion from old-time bull rider H. O. Johnson, who believed Number 11 was the best bull he'd seen since a bull named Red Lightning, of the Kelly string in the 1920s.

Palestine was not Denny Flynn's first encounter with Red Lightning. In their first encounter, at the St. Louis rodeo the previous year, Red Lightning had been the victor. Then, at the George Paul Memorial match held at Del Rio, Texas, Denny rode the bull to an 87 score.

"Then I rode him at Belton, Texas over the 4th of July rodeo. I think that time I was like 85 points.

"All the times before, he turned back to the left. I ride right-handed, and I rode him both times before. But this bull, he got real smart and started going back to the right. And he started throwing everybody off. He bucks a lot harder going to the right than he does to the left.

"I don't know if he'd been ridden up til Palestine after he started turning back to the right, or not."

Denny recalled the events leading up to his historic 98 ride: "I went to Elk City, Oklahoma the night before. I was by myself, and I wasn't really wanting to go to Palestine, because it's so far. I for sure wasn't going to drive it.

"But the only way to get a plane connection was to drive from Elk City that night to Tulsa, Oklahoma. I got there in the early hours of the morning, caught a flight to St. Louis, then rented a car and drove on over to Palestine.

"So that gave me a lot of time to think about him.

"I got there a little early. I was walking around, just making up my mind, how he was going to buck, and what I'd do to ride him.

"The first two, three jumps, they would be just like they've always been before. Then when he blowed up and turned back to the right, I'd just have to let it take its course. When I'm riding, I just ride kind of jump for jump. Then you have to go back to just your reactions. Just go from there, and try to make that 8 second whistle.

" 'Course I had myself pumped up pretty good."

Butch Kirby and Joe Bonner were the judges. Both were seasoned bull riders. The bullfighters were Leon Coffee and Mike Moore. Quail Dobbs worked the barrel out in the arena. All of the men moved back from the chute as Denny eased down over Red Lightning. "With Red Lightning, what you have to do is get plumb back away from him—move the barrel and everything—so he just goes out there and doesn't see anything.

"Then, he's really going to buck."

Denny slid up against his gloved hand. His left arm rested on the chute gate. "I like to hang onto the gate until the bull knocks it open with his head. It just kind of sets me up in a position so when he blows out of there, he can't blow out of the box fast enough to beat me out of there."

True to prediction, Red Lightning's head crashed into the gate at the sound of the latch release. The 1,600-pound bull blew high to the left, out into the arena.

Denny Flynn was with him. For two, three jumps the bull bucked straight into the arena, as expected.

"Then, when he blowed up and turned back to the right, well, he just kicked right over his head. It seemed like his front end just dropped out from under him.

"When he hit he whipped me over his right shoulder. It was

good I was right-handed. I just took my hand and shoved it right in the middle of his back.

"Then he kept coming around to the right and moved under me."

As the bull lunged, twisting into the air, the force field was reversed. "When he blows back up, and when he really spins, he wants to throw you plumb to the outside.

"I really had to just loosen my left, outside, foot up. If I didn't, it would just pull me over towards his left shoulder, and he'd have pulled me down on his head.

"So I just loosened up, just threw myself backwards. Just threw my free arm over to my right shoulder . . . really moved over in there. And he came around and picked me up.

"Every round from then on I could never really get a solid hold there. My outside foot . . . I had to keep throwing it back in . . . I had to keep throwing it back in . . . kicking. It was just a struggle to get a hold.

"But you know the next jump is going to be just like the other one.

"My foot would come out, and I'd just keep throwing it back in.

"My right leg would keep sliding up. But I'd keep shoving it back down. I just really tried to mash with my right leg. The upper part of my leg would come up and meet my riding hand. And I'd wedge it in there . . . use it as a brace.

"All this time you've got to keep your legs in . . . because if you ever slide off your rope, ever get any slack in your legs at all, there's nothing you can do to keep from getting whipped down on his head. I was just riding jump for jump. Just reacting.

"What causes him to be so much harder is he really blows in the air and drops and kicks. He really bucks while he's spinning. He'll wad up and explode and turn back all at the same time.

"Both judges said it was one of his best days."

And the announcer, John Hutson, said it looked like Denny

Flynn was just glued to the bull. "You see something like that . . . you won't forget it in your entire life."

I asked John Hutson if Denny Flynn's 98 ride on Red Lightning in 1979 was the highest point in his announcing career.

"One of them," he answered, quietly.

"I guess a high moment in my life was when I turned on the mike when I went through a loss of speech and paralysis."

"I had a stroke," he began, "on October 2nd, in 1977."

"I was paralyzed down the left side, and I had lost the ability to talk.

"On the weekend of November 2nd, I turned on the microphone, and announced another rodeo.

"That December I announced the National Finals Rodeo.

"The Good Lord blessed me. He performed a miracle.

"You just have to get up, and get with it, and get going again.

"But the overall high point in my life," John Hutson continued, "is all the friendships I've made."

What you have when you get there is what you sent on ahead.

Bibliography

Books and Articles

Brown, Barbara J. "Denny Flynn." *Prorodeo Sports News*, 13 June 1979.
———. "It Was A Long Road, But Cooper Made It." *World Of Rodeo*, January 1980.
"Cooper's Back." *World of Rodeo*, January 1980.
Crawford, Bill. "Roy Cooper, A Career In Jeopardy." *Prorodeo Sports News*, 25 June 1979.
Davis, Ray. "Don And Pete Gay Discuss Bull Riding Gear." *Western Horseman*, December 1973, pp. 62–64, 129–32.
Griffith, Beth. "The Reticent Mr. Gay." *Prorodeo Sports News*, 16 April 1980.
Hall, Douglas Kent. *Rodeo*. New York: Ballantine Books, 1976.
Knocke, Ed. "Steiner's Top of The Line Rodeo Productions." *World of Rodeo*, May 1979.
Maltz, Maxwell. *Psychocybernetics*. New York: Pocket Books, 1960.
St. John, Bob. *On Down The Road*. Englewood Cliffs, N.J.: Prentice-Hall, 1977.
"Steiner's 11: Red Lightning." *Prorodeo Sports News*, 29 November 1978.

131

Interviews and Letters

Alexander, Joe. Marysville, California, 21 August 1974, 19 July 1978, 25 September 1978.

Berger, Bob. Lexington, Oklahoma, 14 November 1978.

Beutler, Lynn. Cody, Wyoming, 25 June 1978.

Collins, Larry. Wheatland, Wyoming, 26 September 1978.

Cook, Bob. Clements, California, 17 October 1978.

Cooper, Roy. Durant, Oklahoma, 31 December 1978, 29 January 1979.

Cooper, Tuffy. Monument, New Mexico, 31 December 1978, 16 January 1979.

Cox, Dickie, Meridian, Texas, 8 November 1978.

Doak, George. Fort Worth, Texas, 9 November 1978.

Ferguson, Ira. Miami, Oklahoma, 19 December 1978.

Ferguson, Larry. Miami, Oklahoma, 21 December 1978.

Ferguson, Tom. Miami, Oklahoma, 23 December 1978.

Flynn, Denny. Charleston, Arkansas, 19, 21 November 1980.

Galemba, Ed. Fort Worth, Texas, 8 November 1978.

Gay, Don. Billings, Montana, 16 October 1978

Gay, Neal. Mesquite, Texas, 21 October 1978.

Hamley, David. Pendleton, Oregon, 7 November 1978.

Hutson, John. Billings, Montana, 9 February 1982.

Hyland, Mel. Salmon Arm, British Columbia, 17 October, 17 November 1978.

Ivory, Buster. Cody, Wyoming, 25 June 1978.

Jones, C. R. Lakeside, California, 16, 21 December 1978.

Larsen, Fred. Douglas, Wyoming, 21 December 1978.

Long, Al. Stephensville, Texas, 8 November 1978.

Luman, Ken. Las Vegas, Nevada, 28 December 1978.

Minick, Billy. Saginaw, Texas, 10 November 1978.

Munroe, Jimmie Gibbs. Valley Mills, Texas, 4 October 1983.

Quintana, Donnalyn. Redmond, Oregon, 4 January 1979.

Quintana, John. Redmond, Oregon, 7, 26 November 1978.

Rodriguez, Jim, Jr., San Luis Obispo, California, 28 December 1978, 1, 14 January 1979, 21 July 1980.

Van Zandt, D. L., D.V.M. Hardin, Montana, 5 October 1983.

Young, Olin. Peralta, New Mexico, 1, 9, 19 January 1979.

Index

Bots Sots Stampede, 1, 2, 5,
7, 9, 10, 13
Bowman, John, 9
Branco, Dan, 68, 70
Breeze Bars, 41
British Columbia, 60
Brooks, Bobby, 11
Brown, Barbara J., 123
Buckskin Billy, 46
Buckshot, 81
Buell, Ralph, 3, 4
Buffalo Bill and the Indians, 13
bulldogging, 12–13, 40, 80.
See also steer wrestling
Bull of the Year, 96, 102, 107,
113, 122, 125
bullriding, 95–107, 109–18,
120, 122–27
bulls, 95–96, 109, 113, 122,
125
Burkburnett, Tex., 5
Buschbom, Jack, 3

calf roping, 7–8, 27, 30–36,
46–48, 61, 80, 81
California, 4, 10, 40, 41, 67,
68, 113
Call, Kenny, 62
Cal Poly, 13, 40
Camarillo, Jerold, 49
Camarillo, Leo, 37–39, 43,
46–50
Camarillo, Reg, 49

Camelot's Broom, 41
Canada, 51, 60
Carey, Andy, 125
Carter, Peter, 28
Casper College, 13
Championship Rodeo
Equipment, 5
Charro, 114
Cheyenne, 3, 9, 11, 51
Cheyenne Frontier Days, 1,
15, 26, 60, 120
Chowchilla, Calif., 68
Clarendon, Tex., 80
Clements, Calif., 113
Cody, Wyo., 17
Cody Bill (Bill Smith), 17–27
Coffee, Leon, 127
coleando, 9
Collins, Larry, 22, 23, 24, 26
Colorado, 16
Colorado State University, 83
Cook, Billy, 31
Cook, Bob, 113, 115
Cooper, Roy, 8, 27–36
Cooper, Tuffy, 31
Copenhaver, Jeff, 46
Cora, Wyo., 17
corriente steer, 13, 68
Cowboy, 70–75
Cowboys Turtle Association,
11
cow cutting, 11
Cow Palace, 114